T0316556

Cambridge Elements

Elements in Public Economics
edited by
Robin Boadway
Queen's University
Frank A. Cowell
The London School of Economics and Political Science
Massimo Florio
University of Milan

THE ECONOMICS AND REGULATION OF NETWORK INDUSTRIES

Telecommunications and Beyond

Ingo Vogelsang†

Boston University

CAMBRIDGE
UNIVERSITY PRESS

CAMBRIDGE
UNIVERSITY PRESS

University Printing House, Cambridge CB2 8BS, United Kingdom

One Liberty Plaza, 20th Floor, New York, NY 10006, USA

477 Williamstown Road, Port Melbourne, VIC 3207, Australia

314–321, 3rd Floor, Plot 3, Splendor Forum, Jasola District Centre,
New Delhi – 110025, India

103 Penang Road, #05–06/07, Visioncrest Commercial, Singapore 238467

Cambridge University Press is part of the University of Cambridge.

It furthers the University's mission by disseminating knowledge in the pursuit of
education, learning, and research at the highest international levels of excellence.

www.cambridge.org
Information on this title: www.cambridge.org/9781108745321
DOI: 10.1017/9781108775410

First published 2021

A catalogue record for this publication is available from the British Library.

ISBN 978-1-108-74532-1 Paperback
ISSN 2516-2276 (online)
ISSN 2516-2268 (print)

The Economics and Regulation of Network Industries

Telecommunications and Beyond

Elements in Public Economics

DOI: 10.1017/9781108775410
First published online: September 2021

Ingo Vogelsang†
Boston University

Editor for correspondence: massimo.florio@unimi.it

Abstract: Have you ever wondered how your telephone company or Internet service provider can give you access to almost all the people in the world or how electricity suppliers can compete with each other if there is only one electric supply line passing through your street? This Element deals with the economics and public regulation of such network industries. It puts particular emphasis on the specific economic concepts used for analyzing them, and on the regulatory reform movement and the compatibility of regulation and competition. Worldwide, most of these industries have changed dramatically in recent years, telecommunications in particular. Network industries mostly exhibit economies of scale in production and similar economies in consumption ('network effects'). Both of these properties cause market power problems that often require industry-specific regulation. However, due to technological and market changes network policies have moved on from end-user regulation to wholesale regulation and, in some cases, to deregulation.

Keywords: network industry, economies of scale and scope, network effects, incentive regulation, deregulation

JEL classifications: L43, L51, L96, L97

ISBNs: 9781108745321 (PB), 9781108775410 (OC)
ISSNs: 2516-2276 (online), 2516-2268 (print)

Contents

1 Introduction

1.1 What Are Network Industries and What Makes Them Interesting Topics in Economics?

The economics and regulation of network industries is an old-fashioned topic that has been totally modernized. What used to be "public utilities" is now called "network industries." This name change signifies both a change in the scope of the relevant industries and a change in their character and of the inquiry into their properties. A typical public utility owned an infrastructure that was made available to end users via regulated monopoly markets. The regulation was justified by a public interest in the services and the required containment of monopoly power. However, regulation was rarely efficient. The resulting critique of traditional regulation naturally induced economists both to recommend deregulation and to look for improvements of regulation.

In a network industry, each company owns a network that is defined by links and nodes. The network connects users with each other. The users can be of the same types, such as in the case of telephone subscribers, or of different types, such as electricity generators and loads or Internet content providers and end users. In the second case, the network acts as a platform that deals with two-sided or multi-sided markets of users. In the Internet age, more and more networks have become interactive rather than being simple distribution networks.

Network industries have several common features that make them challenging and exciting topics of theoretical and empirical inquiry. The combination of the following features means that network industries are subject to various policy interventions.

First, network industries are of vital importance to the economy as infrastructures and "general purpose technologies" (Bresnahan & Trajtenberg, 1995) that the whole population needs and that spill over from individual users to the whole economy. This, for example, justifies universal service policies making the network services available to everyone.

Second, as recognized early on, networks exhibit sunk costs and supply-side economies of scale and scope, which favor large firms supplying many services together. Network industries have therefore traditionally been associated with market power.

Third, a newer subject of inquiry and possibly the reason for the name change from public utility to network industry is the presence of network effects, which are demand-side economies of scale and scope. Without either supply-side or demand-side economies there would be no reason for firms to have networks. They would then link up with each customer individually. Similar to supply-side economies, demand-side economies can lead to market power, but they can also be associated with other allocative distortions. The latter could be the result of direct network effects, which are externalities. For example, a telephone network is worth little if it has only a single subscriber. It gains its value from the presence of many subscribers who can talk to each other. Thus, the decision of a person to become a subscriber benefits others who are not part of that decision. Direct network effects can also be negative, such as in the case of congestion in transport networks, where an additional user increases congestion.

In recent years, indirect network effects have gained increasing importance, largely due to the Internet. Indirect network effects arise from decisions of one type of network user that affect other types of network users. For example, the addition of new newspaper subscribers has a positive effect on advertisers. In the past, due to many subscribers, newspaper subscriptions were cheap, because advertisers largely paid for them. Today they are expensive, because advertisers pay less due to the diminished subscriber base. This is an example of two-sided markets, where the network acts as a platform. The economics of two-sided and multi-sided platforms therefore has a lot in common with the economics of network industries. Since Belleflamme and Peitz (2015) and Comino and Manenti (2014) have skillfully surveyed platforms, we only present some of the main results relevant to network industries and their regulation.

Do all network industries exhibit network effects? Examples outside the telecommunications sector include congestion for transport networks and Kirchhoff's laws for electricity transmission. The expansion of a network may create network effects even in the absence of an increased number of users, although those may join following the expansion. For example, the build-out of a road or railroad system opens up demand opportunities that will attract more users and will usually, but not always, reduce congestion.[1] "If you build it, they will come." These network effects and Kirchhoff's law show the interaction between the supply and the demand side.

While positive network effects favor large network providers, they may also be realized through interconnection between standardized networks. Thus, interconnection and standardization play an important role for network industries and the policies associated with them.

---

[1] The possibility that adding new capacity can increase congestion in a transport network is known as "Braess's Paradox" (Braess, 1969).

A fourth important property of networks is that they generally operate in service industries, which means that their services are consumed at the same time they are produced. As a result, services generally cannot be stored.[2] Since networks are capital goods with capacity limits that depend on the amount invested in them, high-capacity utilization is essential for their profitability. This can, among others, be accomplished through time-dependent pricing techniques and technology choices that reflect the time duration a particular capacity is being used. Furthermore, price discrimination and sophisticated pricing techniques are more appropriate and more easily used in service industries than otherwise.

1.2 The Relationship between Networks and the Services Provided over Them

Networks can be used for the provision of various (goods or) services, such as telephony, cable TV and data services for modern (tele-)communications networks. The networks themselves are the infrastructures over which services are delivered. The networks often require public resources, such as airwaves or rights of way, and have to be managed either by themselves or by public agencies, such as air traffic controllers.

Because of the complementarity of the networks and the services provided over them, the issue of vertical integration vs. separation has arisen. When networks as particular industries first evolved, they were usually vertically integrated in the sense that they produced the inputs necessary for the service provision, and transported the services over the network and sold them to end users. For electricity network providers, this meant that they generated electricity, transported it over the electricity network and sold it at retail. Relative to the network as the core activity, this meant that generation as the upstream activity was integrated, as was retail as the downstream activity. Over time, in electricity, two separate core network activities emerged in the form of transmission and distribution networks, which transport electricity at different voltage levels and over different distances. Similarly, telecommunications networks included long-distance and local networks with different economic properties. Railroads used to be vertically integrated by including the rail tracks, stations and the trains and equipment.

Vertical integration can possess efficiency advantages that make such institutional arrangements more efficient than vertical separation. However, since

---

[2] Note that goods, such as natural gas, which flow over networks can be stored, while the transportation service of the pipeline system cannot. The storage of such goods can, however, substitute for the infeasible storage of the transport service.

core networks mostly exhibit strong economies of scale and scope, while the upstream and downstream activities often do not, competition may be possible for the noncore activities. The advantages of competition on these production stages may then have to be traded off against the disadvantages of vertical separation associated with such competition for the noncore activities.

There are two additional complications in the new developments in network industries. The first is that some of the core activities have exhausted or no longer exhibit economies of scale and therefore can be duplicated without too much loss of production efficiencies. The more this is true, the less there is a policy case for vertical separation (for given vertical economies). The second is that noncore activities, such as "over the top" (OTT) services by nonnetwork owners that are provided over the public Internet, can (a) gain bottleneck properties and/or (b) can compete against activities of network providers.

Based on the strong presence of economies of scale and scope and of network effects, the traditional provision of network industries has been by monopolies with vertical integration of network infrastructure and services. Networks in many countries were state-owned, such as telephone, electricity, gas, water and railroad networks. Today, network industries are characterized by general competition for services and some competition for network infrastructure. Vertically integrated firms compete alongside vertically separated firms, which often depend on essential network inputs from the integrated networks.

Current hot topics in network industries include the emergence of smart electricity distribution grids, electricity storage, net neutrality for Internet service provision of content, the sharing economy, over-the-top services (OTT) in (tele-)communications networks, and the emergence of 5G in mobile communications. We put special emphasis on the telecommunications sector, because it has all the network features and is the most researched network industry. This Element focuses on some models and applications and does not extensively cover the empirical and policy literature.

1.3 Relevant Economic Policies

Network industries have been subject to many policy interventions. The current Element takes a normative approach to such policies but recognizes that there can be conflicts between the normative and the positive approach, which can be relevant for policy recommendations (Briglauer et al., 2019). Since we concentrate on specific industries, only microeconomic policies are of concern.

The main policy issues for network industries concern market power and externalities/network effects. Most countries use two types of policies for dealing with market power. They are competition policy (antitrust), as the general policy relevant for all industries, and economic (industry-specific) regulation, which specializes on particular industries. There exist also two types of policies dealing with externalities: social regulation as the general policy relevant for all industries and industry-specific regulation that sometimes can be combined with economic regulation. Examples of industry-specific policies dealing both with market power and network effects are interconnection regulation for telephony, net neutrality regulation of Internet service providers (ISPs); and radio spectrum regulation for mobile networks, TV and other services.

Competition policy governs all industries, trying to preserve and enhance competition in markets, usually for the long-term benefits of consumers. Competition is threatened by market power, collusion and fraudulent behavior. The relevance of competition policy to network industries is mostly concentrated on issues of monopolization, foreclosure, predation, tying/bundling and mergers. Collusion is currently not a big issue for network industries but that may change. In particular, coinvestment and asset sharing to lower costs are currently hot topics in telecommunications, and they can be associated with collusion between the partners of such undertakings (Krämer & Vogelsang, 2016). The importance of competition policy increases with the increase in competition in network industries and with the increase in the complexity of network industry structures. There is no policy void if industry-specific regulation is abandoned. In particular, competition policy is the fallback in case of deregulation. This happens with the advance of competition in telecommunications and to some degree in electricity. Interestingly, through these developments, competition policy is becoming more "regulatory" (Geradin & Sidak, 2005). Sometimes overlaps or conflicts occur between competition policy and regulation. Most relevant in this regard has been the 2004 US Supreme Court case *Verizon v. Trinko*, where Court ruled against allowing an overlap.[3]

Since industry-specific regulation of private enterprises in its modern form was first practiced in the USA, and since other countries have adapted to it, we put particular emphasis on the US model and briefly touch upon the European Union (EU), India and China.

US regulation is performed by "independent" commissions. Independent here means that the regulatory agency is somewhat independent of the government and has some executive, legislative and judiciary powers. The regulatory agency is headed by commissioners, who are supported by a sometimes-large staff. Commissioners can be appointed by the head of government or elected by popular vote. There are federal and state commissions for the regulated network

---

[3] *Verizon Communications v. Law Offices of Curtis V. Trinko, LLP, 540 U.S. 398* (2004).

industries. Federal commissioners are appointed by the US President and confirmed by the Senate, while state commissioners can either be appointed by the Governor or be elected. The number of staff members varies between 3 for small state commissions and 2,500 for large federal commissions, such as the Federal Energy Regulatory Commission (FERC) or the Federal Communications Commission (FCC).

The division of labor between federal and state commissions is guided by the Commerce Clause and the Supremacy Clause of the US Constitution. The Commerce Clause makes sure that activities that directly concern several states (inter-state commerce) are dealt with at the federal level, while activities concerning a single state (intra-state commerce) are dealt with at that state level. While this sounds like a clear rule, it can be quite fuzzy for network industries that are interconnected across states.

The Supremacy Clause allows Congress to pass laws that concern the whole USA, even if each activity is restricted to single states. This has, for example, occurred when the Telecommunications Act of 1996 regulated wholesale access to local telephone lines. This was done in order to have a unified approach across the country.

The regulatory activities can be classified into adjudication and rulemaking. Under adjudication, the commissioners will decide about a single case, which can be an application by the regulated firm for a price increase or the complaint of an electricity generator that a transmission network has refused to interconnect with it. In contrast, rulemaking concerns the development of new policies because of new technological and market developments. In both cases, adjudication and rulemaking, the regulatory agency can have a fair amount of discretion in its decision-making. This property of regulation is meant to allow the regulators to deal with new and/or contentious issues in a nonpolitical, nonpartisan way. This discretion is limited by the regulatory statute that prescribes what the agency can do and what its guiding purpose is and, very importantly, by due process. The latter is guided by the Administrative Procedures Act. It makes sure that the regulators give all stakeholders the public opportunity to participate in the preparations that lead to the regulatory decisions. This also allows interested parties to challenge the regulatory decisions in court. In fact, courts up to the US Supreme Court have had immense influence on US industry-specific regulation.

Regulators exercise control over the regulated firms via behavioral or structural interventions. Behavioral interventions are usually less drastic. They primarily concern the prices and profits the regulated firms can achieve, where the main control variable in the past has been the allowed rate of return on the firm's invested capital. Another important area of regulatory control concerns entry, exit and investment. Firms often may not simply start a regulated business and those already under regulation may not simply leave it. Very often, regulated firms have to share their investment plans with the regulator and have them approved. A third area of regulatory concern is that of quality of service. This often takes the form of an obligation to serve or of a common carrier obligation. An obligation to serve means that the regulated firm has to hold enough capacity to serve and has to serve everybody. In contrast, a common carrier obligation means that the company has to serve everybody indiscriminately. Thus, a common carrier obligation is compatible with full trains or buses that can only serve a limited number of people, as long as they do not favor some users over others.

Structural regulation concerns, in particular, horizontal and vertical separation of integrated firms. As indicated, these are very drastic interventions, since they split up going concerns. For that reason, instead of true legal vertical separation, accounting separation is often used in order to preserve some of the economies of scope while still achieving resolutions to conflict of interest problems vis-à-vis vertically separated competitors.

While the US regulatory regime evolved in a contentious political and legal process without any advance planning, the EU established planned regulatory approaches in some of the network industries, in telecommunications in particular. These approaches tried to assure a free flow of services across EU member states associated with free entry of firms in the member states. Thus, even without having a central regulatory EU agency, the EU stipulated regulatory rules, within which the national regulatory agencies (NRAs) had to operate. Similar to the US regulatory commissions, the NRAs are now also largely independent of their governments and are guided by industry-specific laws and due process. Industry-specific regulation in Australia and New Zealand has the special feature that the regulators are part of the agency that also guards competition policy. In Australia, it is the Australian Competition and Consumer Commission (ACCC) and in New Zealand the New Zealand Commerce Commission (NZCC).

India and China, as the countries with the World's largest number of wireless connections, have both started from the traditional ministerial-bureaucratic decision-making model but moved from there in different directions (Liu & Jayakar, 2012). Both countries had to deal with interest group problems and international pressures but responded differently. While India embraced private enterprises and followed a traditional regulatory approach, China kept telecommunications carriers under public ownership. In both cases, political pressures remain so that the Indian regulatory set up is not as independent as in the other countries discussed previously. Liu and Jayakar (2012) characterize the Indian approach as incremental, litigious, and influenced by fractious interest groups.

In contrast, the Chinese policy approach is more influenced from the macro level and likely to be nonincremental. In particular, China has early on recognized the importance of telecommunications for economic growth and has therefore pushed technological and market advances. The remarkable property of the Chinese approach is the parallel existence of several telecommunications carriers owned by the central state. How these companies with common ownership compete with each other is certainly worth an academic investigation. Xia (2017) points out that China has specifically promoted competition, while containing private participation in network operations and that it has been able to separate ownership from regulatory functions in government. Liu and Jayakar (2012) do, however, emphasize the paradoxical regulator-owner interface. In contrast to the network infrastructure provision, service providers such as mobile virtual network operators (MVNOs) and telecommunications equipment manufacturing are allowed to be in private hands.

1.4 Overview

The next section develops specific economic concepts associated with network industries. It is followed in Section 3 by regulatory approaches based on monopoly. These sections concentrate on monopoly, in spite of the fact that competition today is present in all network industries. However, monopolistic bottlenecks persist in core areas. The economic and regulatory treatment of these core areas is more complex and builds on insights from the simple monopoly approach, which therefore comes first. Section 4 analyzes those competitive developments and their regulatory treatment. Section 5 addresses some special issues of telecommunications. Section 6 deals with the current and upcoming issue of deregulation. Section 7 concludes.

2 Economic Concepts Associated with Network Industries

Because of the specific economic features of network industries, a number of economic concepts have been developed for their study. Although these concepts have general applicability throughout the economy, they were developed here first and have found their widest application in network industries. These concepts refer to costs and demands. This section also includes the resulting welfare concepts for a normative analysis.

2.1 Single-Product Cost Concepts

The first major cost concept concerns economies of scale, which define the cost advantage of large networks over small networks and lead to natural monopolies in a single-product setting. Second, there are various concepts associated with networks as multiproduct firms. These concepts include incremental costs and stand-alone costs, which are necessary for defining economies of scope and cross-subsidies. Together with economies of scale, economies of scope lead to natural monopolies in a multiproduct setting. The concept of average cost, which helps define economies of scale in the single-product case, is no longer well defined for multiproduct firms and is therefore replaced by ray-average costs.

Under a single-product firm, economies of scale mean per unit cost advantages from producing more of the same product; that is, average cost declines as the output increases,

$$\frac{dAC(Q)}{dQ} < 0.$$

Here 'Q' stands for the quantity of output and 'AC' for average cost. Also, under economies of scale, the elasticity of cost w.r.t. output, σ_C, is less than 1,

$$\frac{MC}{AC} = \sigma_c = \frac{dC(Q)}{C(Q)} \Big/ \frac{dQ}{Q} < 1.$$

Here C(Q) is the cost function and MC stands for marginal cost. If $\sigma_c = 1$, there are constant costs or constant returns of scale. If the inequality is reversed, there are diseconomies of scale.

Where do scale economies come from? It is easy to envisage a constant cost industry, where a doubling of all inputs leads to doubling of output. However, both economies of scale and diseconomies of scale are harder to explain. There are four common explanations for economies of scale. First, some inputs come in lumps. Such indivisible inputs lead to downward-sloping average cost curves over some range, until the input reaches its capacity. Then, as output increases, another indivisible input has to be added, leading to a jump in average cost and then again to declines. As output increases further, this leads to average cost ratcheting with declining peaks. A second explanation for economies of scale is the 2/3 rule for the relationship between surface and volume of containers. This holds, for example, for ducts that carry fibre-optic cables. Here the 2/3 rule would apply to the size of ducts, while lumpiness and sunk costs hold for laying the ducts in the ground. The third and most common advantage is the division of labor made famous by Adam Smith. A fourth explanation concerns quantity rebates on input prices. This also alerts to the fact that economies of scale and returns to scale are related but not the same concepts. Economies of scale are a cost concept, while returns to scale are a production function concept. This explanation naturally begs the question where these quantity rebates come from. Here again economies of scale can be a major reason, while buying power could be another.

What are the specific reasons for economies of scale in network industries? First, networks are composed of links and nodes that tend to be capital goods with lumpy characteristics. Second, networks have to either link subscribers to a source or several sources or to each other. Switched nodes then allow for savings on links so that the total number of links can be much smaller than if every subscriber were directly linked to the source or to each other. These savings increase dramatically in a factorial way with the number of subscribers.

For networks, a related concept to economies of scale are economies of density. Such economies relate to the fact that for a given number of subscribers the cost of a network with smaller geographic coverage will have lower cost. Thus, a telephone network in a densely populated city will have lower cost per subscriber than a network in a large rural area with the same number of subscribers. The network links in the city will simply be shorter (although this could be compensated for by higher real estate prices and wages in the city).

Although economies of scale and sunk costs are in principle independent of each other, economies of scale in network industries are commonly associated with sunk costs, such as those incurred by digging up the ground for installing ducts or lines. Sunk costs are defined by the property that the costs of an input, once they have been spent, cannot be recovered other than by using the input for the particular dedicated output. In other words, there is no functioning second-hand market for the particular input. The sunk cost property increases the risk and thereby the cost of investment and can create a barrier to entry.

2.2 Single-Product Natural Monopoly Concepts

Closely related but not identical to economies of scale is the natural monopoly property. In the traditional view, it attempts to answer the question of what the cost-minimizing market structure is. This *supply-side natural monopoly* (= *classic natural monopoly*) means that total costs of industry output is less when produced by a single firm than by any number 'N' of firms greater than one. In other words, it's cheaper to produce all the outputs in a single firm than in more than one firm. A firm represents a *natural monopoly* if its cost function is *sub-additive* over all relevant outputs,

$$C\left(\sum_{i=1}^{N} Q_i\right) < \sum_{i=1}^{N} C(Q_i), N \geq 2.$$

The classic natural monopoly is clearly caused by cost advantages of being large. However, natural monopoly can still exist even if there are diseconomies of scale (or scope) over some range of output(s). If this range is sufficiently small, a single firm will have lower cost of the total market output than two or more firms, each of which does do not exhaust its scale economies.

While the classic natural monopoly is described in all textbooks on public utility regulation, a newer demand-related natural monopoly concept is rarely mentioned, although it is of potentially major importance for modern network industries. Direct and indirect network effects have been called *demand-side economies of scale* (Shapiro & Varian, 1999). They can give rise to a *demand-side natural monopoly*. Such a natural monopoly characterizes the consumer-surplus-maximizing market structure at a given price. It is associated with a *super-additive* demand function (versus the *sub-additive* cost function for supply-side determinants of natural monopoly). It is related to endogenous sunk costs, which are global and grow with market size. Super-additive demand is relevant for Internet-related industries, such as social networks.

The demand-side natural monopoly was first defined by Shaffer (1983). Begin by defining the inverse demand function $P(Q)$ to be strictly super-additive if and only if for all firms i and for $Q = \sum_{i=1}^{N} Q_i$:

$$P(Q) > \sum_{i=1}^{N} P(Q_i), Q_i > 0, N \geq 2 .$$

This condition says that consumers are willing to pay a higher price for an amount Q of a commodity if it is produced by a single firm than if it is produced by any combination of two or more firms. From this follows that a single-product industry with constant returns to scale is a strict (demand-side) natural monopoly if and only if its inverse demand function is strictly super-additive. A sufficient condition for super-additivity is that average revenue (or inverse demand) increases in scale (Shapiro & Varian, 1999). This can happen if positive network effects from an increased subscribership outweigh the price effects of an otherwise downward-sloping demand.

The downward-sloping thin inverse demand curves $P(Q,Q_i)$ in Figure 1 represent market demands as a function of price for a given expected number of subscribers, Q_i. The demands shift outward as i increases. The expectations, however, are only fulfilled where $Q_i = Q$. Linking these points of fulfilled demands yields the fulfilled expectations demand, which over some range is upward-sloping.[4] In this upward-sloping part, the network effect of increasing demand is stronger than the conventional law of decreasing demand. As more subscribers have joined the network, the network effect decreases, leading to a downward-sloping segment of the fulfilled expectations demand.

---

[4] This insight originally goes back to Rohlfs (1974). See also Mitchell & Vogelsang (1991).

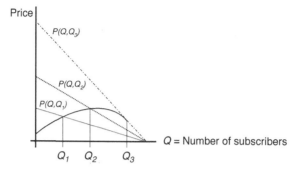

Figure 1 Fulfilled expectations demand

In principle, for many prices there exist two quantities that could be market outcomes. The equilibrium points in the upward-sloping portion of the fulfilled expectations demand are unstable, while those in the downward-sloping portion are stable. Unstable here means that if the actual demand turns out to be higher (lower) than expected, a new equilibrium will result with a higher (lower) number of demanded subscriptions than before, which means that the number of subscribers will again be underestimated (overestimated). Overall, market participants would have an interest in settling for points in the downward-sloping section of demand, which may require coordination in the form of nudging or some financial incentives.

Under demand-side natural monopoly (and with no diseconomies of scale in production) a single supplier would be the efficient market structure. However, in reality, consumers typically have heterogeneous tastes regarding networks. Thus, the demand-side economies of scale compete with the benefits of product differentiation if differentiated networks are incompatible with each other. Thus, consumers will weigh the benefits from joining a larger network with those from joining a network that is more to their taste. If the network externalities are stronger than the perceived benefits of product differentiation then there may still exist a demand-side natural monopoly. Furthermore, demand-side economies and supply-side economies may come together, thereby potentially creating strong natural monopoly conditions. Google's search engine may be a case in point. Even if network services are homogeneous, a demand-side natural monopoly does not require monopoly provision if interconnection between networks or multi-homing is feasible and cheap.

2.3 Relevant Concepts for Multiproduct Firms

Although microeconomics concentrates on single-product firms, the economy is actually dominated by multiproduct firms. In fact, it is hard to name any single-product firms. Even firms that seem to produce a single homogeneous product usually offer different varieties of it. In contrast, all the common enterprises around us are multiproduct firms. This holds, in particular, for services such as those offered by network industries. Why are multiproduct firms particularly common in service industries that seem to offer homogeneous products like electricity? Services are typically already differentiated by time and location. Because it cannot be stored, electricity sold during the day is no close substitute for electricity sold during the night. Likewise, a telephone call between cities A and B is no close substitute for a call between cities C and D.

Multiproduct firms require a special approach to profit maximization and welfare maximization, because different products have costs in common and because their demands interact. For example, the average-cost concept developed for single-product firms does not work for multiproduct firms. Why? It is because average cost cannot be defined fully generally, since output now is a vector and one cannot divide total cost by several different output quantities (or divide a scalar by a vector). How then do we define average costs for these firms? One needs a more restricted definition. The first and most relevant of these concepts is called *ray average cost* (RAC). Assume the total cost for a two-product firm is $C(Q_1, Q_2)$, meaning that the firm makes two products, *1* and *2* with the quantities q_1 and q_2. Further assume that the two outputs are produced in a constant ratio $\varsigma_1 : \varsigma_2$, *s.t.* $\varsigma_1 + \varsigma_2 = 1$. Then the set of outputs is defined implicitly from the equations $Q_1 = \varsigma_1 Q$ *and* $Q_2 = \varsigma_2 Q$. Ray average cost is now defined as:

$$RAC(Q) = \frac{C(\varsigma_1 Q, \varsigma_2 Q)}{Q}.$$

RAC assumes that outputs are produced in fixed proportions. The RAC can vary for every product ratio and product level. Thus, RAC captures average costs along a ray from the origin. Further on, we will define the simpler concept of average incremental cost.

As in the single-product case, economies of scale for multiple products relates to (ray) average cost. If we increase all outputs proportionally, say by a factor of v, then multiproduct economies of scale are defined by

$$\frac{\partial RAC(vQ)}{\partial v} < 0.$$

This means that we have decreasing ray average cost. In this case, multiplying by v makes the output proportions stay the same.

In contrast to average cost, the marginal cost for product i of a multiproduct firm is well-defined as

$$MC_i = \frac{\partial C(Q_1, Q_2)}{\partial Q_i}, \quad i = 1, 2.$$

Very useful concepts for costing and pricing in network industries are *incremental cost* and *stand-alone cost*. Again, consider the two-product case with total cost: $C(Q_1, Q_2)$.

The *stand-alone cost* is then defined as the cost of only producing one product:

$$SAC(Q_1) = C(Q_1, 0), \quad SAC(Q_2) = C(0, Q_2).$$

In contrast, the incremental cost is the cost of adding a product if the firm is already producing one product.

Thus, the incremental cost of product *1* is the total cost minus stand-alone cost of the other product *2*.

$$IC(Q_1) = C(Q_1, Q_2) - C(0, Q_2).$$

If a producer starts producing only product *2*, then the incremental cost of product *1* can be interpreted as the extra cost the producer has to incur if he starts to produce both products.

The *average incremental cost* of product *1* now is defined as:

$$AIC(q_1) = \frac{C(Q_1, Q_2) - C(0, Q_2)}{Q_1}.$$

Declining AIC defines *product-specific* economies of scale:

$$\frac{\partial AIC(Q_1)}{\partial Q_1} < 0.$$

A very useful concept characterizing the economies achieved by having multi-product rather than single-product firms is that of *economies of scope*. Economies of scope mean that it is cheaper to produce a number of different products together than separately. They are also called synergies.[5]

In the two-product case, *economies of scope* exist if the sum of stand-alone costs is greater than total cost:

---

[5] Such synergies can also induce separate firms to share assets or to coinvest rather than to merge fully.

$$SAC(Q_1) + SAC(Q_2) > C(Q_1, Q_2).$$

Since

$$C(Q_1, Q_2) = C(0, Q_2) + IC(Q_1),$$

it follows from the definitions of stand-alone cost and incremental cost that

$$C(0, Q_2) + C(Q_1, 0) > C(0, Q_2) + IC(Q_1).$$

Thus, in the presence of economies of scope, the stand-alone cost of a product is greater than its incremental cost.

$$SAC(Q_1) > IC(Q_1).$$

As in the single-product case, natural monopoly means that total cost of the industry output is less when produced by a single firm than by any number of firms greater than one. Now, however, the industry consists of multiple products. Equally, it is cheaper to produce all the products in a single firm than in more than one firm. A firm then is a classic natural monopoly if its cost function is sub-additive,

$$C\left(\sum_{i=1}^{n} Q_i\right) < \sum_{i=1}^{N} C(Q_i), N \geq 2.$$

In the multiproduct case, Q_i is a vector: $Q_i = (Q_{1i}, Q_{2i}, \ldots, Q_{mi})$.

The combination of economies of scale and economies of scope for any vector of the firm's outputs is sufficient for the existence of a multiproduct natural monopoly. However, analogous to the case of single-product monopoly, such a natural monopoly can still exist, even if there are diseconomies of scale or scope over some range of outputs.

2.4 Consumer Surplus as Part of a Welfare Measure

Following a widespread tradition in regulatory economics, we use consumer surplus as part of our welfare measure along with the profits of the relevant firm(s). While the resulting social surplus = consumer surplus + profits is an impure measure that, in particular, neglects income effects and the distributional effects of price changes, it is highly convenient and easy to interpret. In the single-product case, consumer surplus = $CS(P)$ measures the consumer willingness to pay a product at price P. Thus, we measure consumer surplus as the demand area above the price that the firm charges. In the multiproduct case, consumer surplus = $V(P)$ is used more in the sense of indirect utility. Consumer surplus in the multiproduct case is easily defined for the case of products that are independent in demands. In this case the multiproduct consumer surplus is simply the sum of the single-product consumer surpluses. Thus, in the multi-product case, if products are independent from each other (cross elasticity is zero), then

$$V(\boldsymbol{P}) = \sum_{i=1}^{N} CS(P_i).$$

In general this, however, no longer holds if the products are substitutes and/or complements. If the cross elasticities do not equal zero, we have to consider the effect of a price change of P_i on $CS(P_j)$, $i \neq j$. In that case the change of the price of one product shifts the demand for the other product(s). Thus, these shifts generate further consumer surplus additions or reductions that have to be taken into consideration. Since these additional changes in general depend on the order in which price changes are done, the multiproduct consumer surplus very often is no longer unique (i.e., it is path dependent). It is only unique if the cross-derivatives of demand for goods i and j are the same as between goods j and i. This holds if there are no income effects.

2.5 Welfare Benchmarks for Policies

For establishing a simple welfare benchmark in monopoly, we assume a static, single product, and a full information environment.

As indicated previously, the regulator maximizes *social surplus* with respect to price, which results in price equaling marginal cost:

$$\max_{P} W(P) = \pi(P) + CS(P) = PQ - C(Q) + \int_{\tilde{P}}^{\infty} Q(P)dP$$

$$F.O.C. \ w.r.t. \ P: \quad Q + P\frac{\partial Q}{\partial P} - \frac{\partial C(Q)}{\partial Q}\frac{\partial Q}{\partial P} - Q = 0$$

$$\Rightarrow \quad \left(P - \frac{\partial C(Q)}{\partial Q}\right)\frac{\partial Q}{\partial P} = 0$$

$$\Rightarrow \quad P = MC.$$

However, due to economies of scale, $P = MC \rightarrow P < AC$. Thus, in order to achieve the optimal price, the regulator would have to *subsidize* the firm to make up for the loss. However, several problems may arise from using a subsidy in order to achieve efficient pricing. First, a subsidy may give the firm wrong incentives such that the firm has little motivation to lower its cost. Second, the total consumer willingness to pay may be less than the cost of production. Third, and particularly important, the subsidy comes from the government, which raises money through taxes, through profits of state-owned firms, by issuing debt, or through inflation (by printing money). In all these cases, raising the money for the subsidy could create major distortions in other markets thereby causing welfare losses. These losses can be quite high. Thus, by using subsidies, the government is improving the efficiency in one market while creating a potentially much larger inefficiency in another market. Fourth, the availability of subsidies may induce bribes to get them.

Instead, as a result of all these factors, it is preferable for the regulator to maximize net social surplus under a *break-even constraint*. In the single-product case, with economies of scale, this will simply lead to average cost pricing.

In the multiproduct case, where average costs are not well-defined, the policy rule concerning the welfare-maximizing monopoly prices, subject to a constraint on the monopoly's profit being nonnegative, is called *Ramsey pricing*. It is designed to maximize social welfare with the least distortions across markets.

The setup for Ramsey pricing is as follows:

Total cost: $C(Q_1, Q_2, \ldots, Q_N)$.

Demand for each product: $Q_i(P_1, P_2, \ldots, P_N), i = 1, 2, \ldots N$.

We differentiate between the cases of independent and interdependent demands.

Under independent demands, $Q_i(P_1, P_2, \ldots, P_N) = Q_i(P_i)$, for all $i = 1, 2, \ldots N$.

In this case, the regulator's problem becomes

$$\max_{(P_1, P_2, \ldots P_N)} (1 + \mu)\left[\sum_{i=1}^{N} P_i \cdot Q_i - C(Q_1(P_1), Q_2(P_2), \ldots Q_N(P_N))\right]$$

$$+ \sum_{i=1}^{N} CS_i(P_i)$$

$$s.t. \ \pi \geq 0$$

$$\Rightarrow \ Lerner \ Indices \ LI_i \equiv \frac{P_i - \frac{\partial C}{\partial Q_i}}{P_i} = -\frac{\mu}{1 + \mu} \cdot \frac{1}{\varepsilon_i}$$

$$\Rightarrow \ \frac{LI_i}{LI_j} = \frac{\varepsilon_j}{\varepsilon_i}.$$

Thus, in the case of a nonbinding break-even constraint with $\mu = 0$, we get marginal cost pricing. The constraint will be nonbinding if economies of scale are exhausted. The Lagrange multiplier will become infinite if the unconstrained profit-maximizing monopoly will just be able to break even. In general, under Ramsey pricing with independent demands and a binding constraint, the ratio of markups of any two products equals the inverse ratio of their elasticities. If a product has the relatively higher (lower) absolute value of the elasticity, then its price markup should be lower (higher).

In contrast, under interdependent demand, we have $Q_i = Q_i(P_1, P_2, \ldots P_N)$, $i = 1, 2, \ldots N$.

Note here that one cannot add consumer surpluses separately. Thus, in this case, the regulator's problem becomes

$$\max_{(P_1, P_2, \ldots P_N)} \mathcal{L} = (1+\mu)\left[\sum_{i=1}^{N} P_i \cdot Q_i - C(Q_1, Q_2, \ldots Q_N)\right]$$
$$+ V(P_1, P_2, \ldots P_N)$$

$$s.t. \ \pi \geq 0$$

$$F.O.C. \ w.r.t. \ P_i:$$

$$\frac{\partial \mathcal{L}}{\partial P_i} = (1+\mu)\left[Q_i(P_1, \ldots P_N) + \sum_{j=1}^{N} P_j \cdot \frac{\partial Q_j}{\partial P_i} - \sum_{j=1}^{N} \frac{\partial C}{\partial Q_j} \cdot \frac{\partial Q_j}{\partial P_i}\right]$$
$$- Q_i(P_1, \ldots P_N) = 0$$

$$\Rightarrow Lerner \ Indices \ L_i \ with \quad LI_i \equiv \frac{P_i - \frac{\partial C}{\partial Q_i}}{P_i} = -\frac{\mu}{1+\mu} \cdot \frac{1}{\eta_i}.$$

Here η_i is the *super elasticity* of product i. Super elasticities are combinations of direct and cross elasticities that capture the direct and indirect effects of price changes. The super elasticities for a two-product case are as follows. Denote $\varepsilon_k = \frac{\partial Q_k}{\partial P_k} \cdot \frac{P_k}{Q_k} =$ ordinary elasticity and $\varepsilon_{kl} = \frac{\partial Q_k}{\partial P_l} \cdot \frac{P_l}{Q_k} =$ cross elasticity.
Then

$$\eta_1 = \varepsilon_1 \frac{\varepsilon_1 \varepsilon_2 - \varepsilon_{21} \varepsilon_{12}}{\varepsilon_1 \varepsilon_2 + \varepsilon_1 \varepsilon_{12}}$$
$$\eta_2 = \varepsilon_2 \frac{\varepsilon_1 \varepsilon_2 - \varepsilon_{21} \varepsilon_{12}}{\varepsilon_1 \varepsilon_2 + \varepsilon_2 \varepsilon_{21}}.$$

The sign of η_i can be either positive or negative. To see this, consider the two-product case: If the two products are *substitutes* and we increase P_1 then, due to the substitution effect, Q_2 increases. This usually leads to a higher optimal Ramsey markup for that particular good. If the two products are *complements*, increasing P_1 lowers Q_2. This usually leads to a lower optimal Ramsey markup for that particular good. The existence of complements is a necessary, but not sufficient, condition for super elasticities to be negative. Negative super elasticities would lead to negative Ramsey markups for those services. This possibility is closely related to the well-known similar result in two-sided markets.

3 Regulatory Approaches Based on Monopoly Provision

Monopoly provision appears to be desirable in the presence of economies of scale and scope and of demand-side economies covering the whole market(s). It has been the traditional market structure of many network industries. The previously developed marginal cost prices and Ramsey prices represent idealized optimal regulation benchmarks.

In contrast, we now consider more realistic approaches applicable to the practice in the form of rate-of-return regulation and incentive regulation. Incentive regulation acknowledges regulatory imperfections, moving from *optimal* regulation in the direction of *practical* regulation with desirable properties.

3.1 Rate-of-Return Regulation

The traditional approach to monopoly regulation in the USA is known as rate-of-return regulation. In contrast to our approach so far, it did not emerge as the result of optimizing behavior (i.e., not welfare maximization) but rather from political and fairness considerations. In particular, the practice has been sanctioned by a US Supreme Court decision (*Federal Power Commission v. Hope Natural Gas*, known as the "Hope" decision; January 3, 1944).[6] This has provided it with substantial commitment power, as a result of which rate-of-return regulation has survived to this day.

The basic questions posed in the traditional US policy debate have been: how much should the firm be allowed to earn under regulation and what prices are "just and reasonable"? The answers to both of these have led to a cost justification of prices. More specifically, a differentiation has been made between the so-called *revenue requirement* and the so-called *rate design*.

The revenue requirement (price level) concerns the question: how much should a firm benefit relative to the consumers? In contrast, the rate design (price structure/relative prices) concerns the question: how much should prices differ among different consumer groups or among different products?

Under the revenue requirement, the firm's revenue should be able to cover its accounting cost so that

$$R = \sum_{i=1}^{N} P_i Q_i = current\ expenses + D_t + \left(K - \sum_{t=0}^{i} D_t\right) * s,$$

---

[6] FEDERAL POWER COMMISSION et al. v. HOPE NATURAL GAS CO. CITY OF CLEVELAND v. SAME, 320 U.S. 591 (64 S.Ct. 281, 88 L.Ed. 333) Nos. 34 and 35.

where

$D_{\hat{t}}$ = depreciation for period $\hat{t}$

Current expenses $+ D_{\hat{t}}$ = *operating costs*

K = original investment, price of the asset

$\sum_{t=0}^{\hat{i}} D_t$ = sum of depreciation in the past

$\left(K - \sum_{t=0}^{\hat{i}} D_t \right)$ = "rate base" or RAB = regulatory asset base;

s = allowed rate of return, $s \geq r$

r = opportunity cost of financing the investment contained in the rate base = required rate of return to make the firm whole.

All these cost items have to be measured by the regulatory agency. The resulting accounting cost differs from the cost used in the previous sections by the property that they are not necessarily on the cost function, which measures minimum costs of outputs.

Current expenses are the most straightforward component of the revenue requirement. They simply include how much the firm has paid for inputs that are used up in the current period. However, the questionable still remains if these purchases were necessary and efficient and if they were used to produce the regulated output, not something else.

$D_{\hat{t}}, \sum_{t=0}^{\hat{i}} D_t$: Depreciation is the change in economic value for capital assets. This is known as "economic" depreciation. However, $D_{\hat{t}}$ might differ for different depreciation methods (due to different purposes and different parties' interests). Economic depreciation is hard to measure if there are no good second-hand markets for the assets in question. Tax depreciation is mostly linear and based on expected life of asset types. Regulators will often use their own depreciation methods, which again differ from economic and from tax depreciation.

The allowed rate of return has been the most problematic part of the revenue requirement to measure. Since revenues should properly cover the cost of the firm, the allowed rate of return should be closely related to the cost of financing assets, which leads us to the question: How should we measure those costs? We concentrate on firm i's *required rate of return* r_i on the rate base $\left(K - \sum_{t=0}^{\hat{i}} D_t \right)$. Here r_i is usually defined as the *WACC* (weighted average cost of capital). It averages over the *cost of debt* (r_i^d) and the *cost of equity* (r_i^e).

Debt is a contractual obligation. The cost of debt is the overall rate paid for the various types of debt (bond, loan) issued by the firm. Generally,

$$r_i^d = r_f + r_i^p.$$

Here r_i^p is the firm-specific risk premium of firm i, r_f is the risk free rate and r_i^d should equal the yield of the firm's bonds.

Equity has no contractual costs associated with it. Rather, the cost of equity is the shareholders' required return on firm i's existing securities (shares of equity). Since the shareholders are the residual claimants, they face more risk than the bondholders, therefore, $r_i^e > r_i^d$.

Assuming that shareholders diversify, the Capital Asset Pricing Model (CAPM) is commonly used to calculate the return:

$$r_i^e = r_f + \beta_i \left(E(r_m) - r_f \right).$$

$E(r_m)$: expected stock market return

$$\beta_i = \frac{cov\left(r_i^e, r_m\right)}{var(r_m)}$$

$\beta_i > 1$, adding firm i's stock to the portfolio increases the market risk
$0 < \beta_i \leq 1$, reduction of market risk
$\beta_i \leq 0$, hedge the market risk.

Firm-specific or so-called *idiosyncratic* risk, such as the risk from revenue volatility that requires costly liquidity management, is not included in the CAPM and is usually not considered by regulators. It tends to be larger for smaller firms.

One way to determine the allowed rate of return is by equaling it to the cost of capital. Thus, ideally, $s = r = \alpha r^d + (1 - \alpha) r^e$, where α is the weight of debt in total capital. In practice, it is hard to set the allowed rate of return equal to the cost of capital, because the cost of capital can only be measured with uncertainty. As a result, regulators often try to assess the allowed rate of return in terms of the relevant percentiles of the probability distribution of the cost of capital measurements. Historically, regulators seem to have erred in favor of an allowed rate of return in excess of the measured expected cost of capital (Evans & Garber, 1988). This observation has been associated with the so-called "Averch–Johnson" effect, which is the tendency of rate of-return-regulated firms to engage in excessive amounts of capital accumulation in order to expand the volume of their profits (Averch & Johnson, 1962). Therefore, under rate-of-return (and cost-plus) regulation, the firm has no incentives to minimize cost. Rather, it would intentionally increase its cost to earn more profit, which is called "gold plating."

It is hard to measure the Averch–Johnson effect empirically. However, the comparative (to other countries) lack of time-dependent pricing in US electricity and telephone markets under rate-of-return regulation has been taken as an empirical indicator.

While the Averch–Johnson effect introduces an inefficiency, rate-of-return regulation may still be better than no regulation, because the price for consumers will be lower. One way to deal with the A-J problem is to apply a "used-and-useful criterion": The firm is free to build extra plants as long as it remains in the rate-of-return range and the plant can ex post be shown to be used and useful. Such ex post showing, however, creates serious verification and regulatory commitment problems if demand or cost conditions cannot be predicted with certainty (Armstrong & Sappington, 2007).

The rate design concerns the question of how to differentiate prices for different services. The method of pricing the various services associated with rate-of-return regulation is known as *fully distributed cost (FDC) pricing*. To explain, we assume the simple cost function $C = K + c_1Q_1 + c_2Q_2 + \ldots + c_NQ_N$. Here K = common cost and c_i = attributable (incremental or marginal) cost of product i.

Under FDC pricing, the regulator distributes all the costs to the individual products. First, one assigns the directly attributable cost $(c_1, c_2, \ldots c_N)$ to each product. Second, one assigns the nonattributable (common) cost to each individual product by a proportional markup on the directly attributable cost or by a markup based on quantity.

Since these last costs are common, their assignment is somewhat arbitrary. As shown by Braeutigam (1980) and Baumol et al. (1987), fully distributed cost pricing is compatible with any arbitrary price structure. The regulator can use this arbitrariness to burden or favor different groups, which often leads to *cross subsidization*. The standard characterization of cross subsidization contrasts prices with the incremental and stand-alone costs of the services in question as follows (Faulhaber, 1975):

- A customer group (service) is *being subsidized* if its price is below its average incremental cost: $P_j < AIC(Q_j)$.
- A customer group (service) is *subsidizing* if its price is above its average stand-alone cost: $P_j > ASAC(Q_j)$.

Cross subsidization will create a deadweight loss (i.e., a lost welfare triangle) on both the subsidizing and the subsidized sides. From an efficiency perspective, the group or service being subsidized consumes too much, and the group or service subsidizing consumes too little. Cross subsidization has played a large role in monopoly regulation. Regulators often favor some customer groups by burdening others. This works if there is no competition. However, it attracts competition and is at the same time incompatible with competition. Cross subsidization was the Achilles heel of monopoly regulation, when competition became feasible. The rigidity of past regulatory pricing under rate-of-return rate design led to a cross-subsidization trap, because regulated monopolists needed not to change politically popular price structures in response to cost changes. While cross subsidization creates and maintains powerful interest groups backing the status quo, it also plants the seeds for competition in the form of cream skimming. This seed grows particularly strongly if the new technologies lack the natural monopoly properties of the old ones, as has happened, for example, in long-distance telephony.

3.2 Regulation under Asymmetric Information: Incentive Regulation

The welfare economics of monopoly regulation developed in Section 2.5 is based on symmetric full information shared by the regulator and the regulated firm. In particular, it does not capture the effects of asymmetric information between regulator and firm on the resolution of the conflict of interest between the two that led to regulation in the first place. Rate-of-return regulation, while addressing the conflict of interest between the regulated firm and its consumers, also neglects the effects of asymmetric information on the efficiency of the outcome. Regulation under asymmetric information acknowledges that regulators face constraints that can be informational, transactional and/or administrative/political (Laffont & Tirole, 1993).

Informational constraints faced by regulators in particular refer to asymmetric information. For example, the firm's cost is private information that only the firm can fully observe, while the regulator cannot observe some costs, such as those of effort, and cannot observe if costs have been minimized.

Transactional constraints refer to the issue that regulators (and firms and other stakeholders) incur high transaction costs from adjudication, rulemaking, monitoring and enforcement. These constraints also have a direct effect on the scope of asymmetric information, which can be lowered, for example, through monitoring. Given that budgets are limited, regulation has to be imperfect.

Administrative (political) constraints refer to a hodgepodge of issues, including that the regulator's budget is set by politicians (legislature) or that regulators are further restricted by certain legal procedures to follow; by limited tenure of regulators; by limited scope of regulation; and by restrictions on the instruments to be used (e.g., no subsidies) etc. Due-process rules have to be followed because of regulatory discretion.

The academic literature has developed two basic types of approaches, one informationally sophisticated and one informationally simple, which explicitly include asymmetric information and its effects on welfare outcomes of regulation.

The informationally sophisticated or "Bayesian" approach has dominated the theoretical literature. The main early milestones here are Baron and Myerson (1982) and Laffont and Tirole (1986). Informationally demanding mechanisms are often called "Bayesian" because here regulators start with a subjective a priori–type distribution of firms and use Bayesian updating to reach posterior distributions. The purpose is to design mechanisms such that profit maximization by the regulated firm leads to goal fulfilment of the regulator, where the objective is assumed to be social surplus maximization with different weights for consumers and regulated firms.

In contrast, the informationally simple approach has been driven by the application to real-life situations. The resulting mechanisms typically have desirable welfare properties under certain conditions but are not strictly welfare-maximizing. We here only provide the basic insights of both these approaches.[7]

3.2.1 The Bayesian Approach

The Bayesian approach models asymmetric information by use of a subjective probability distribution of types of firms. Although the firm is usually a monopoly, it can be viewed as being drawn from a distribution of types θ of similar firms. The type distribution usually only refers to certain parameters of the firm's profit function, such as a multiplicative effect on cost. Thus, in this case, the cost function is differentiated between types only by this parameter, while all other parameters and the functional form of the profit function are the same for all types.

Under the Bayesian approach, the regulator and the firm have (common) knowledge of the structure of the regulatory problems and of certain functions and parameters (for example, demand and type distribution). In addition, the firm knows something about itself, such as its own type θ or its actions, while the regulator does not. Bayesian regulation is a two-stage game, where in the first stage the regulator proposes a subsidy or tax mechanism, knowing that in the second stage the firm with its superior information is going to maximize its profits net of the subsidy or tax. Welfare itself is a random variable to the regulator.

Bayesian regulation requires complicated mathematical models, even with simplistic functional forms. Yet, major insights can be gained from the simplest models. We here concentrate on two of them as examples. They both use

---

[7] Armstrong & Sappington (2007) provide a much more comprehensive discussion of both Bayesian and simple regulatory mechanisms. They also provide a balanced critique in comparing the two approaches.

weighted welfare functions with lower weights for profits than for consumer welfare. The source of the lower weight can be distributional or it can be based on the costs of public funds that are used for transfers to the firm. The most basic, yet insightful and influential Bayesian regulatory model is by Baron and Myerson (1982). Its main assumptions are the following: The firm's cost function is $C = \theta Q$. The different cost types θ are distributed randomly with a distribution $F(\theta)$ and a density function $f(\theta)$, $\theta \in [\underline{\theta}, \overline{\theta}]$. The firm knows its θ, but the regulator does not. We have

$$\begin{cases} F(\underline{\theta}) = 0 \\ F(\overline{\theta}) = 1 \end{cases}, F'(\theta) = f(\theta) \geq 0.$$

This is a two-stage game. In the first stage, the regulator sets a transfer function $T(P)$. In the second stage, given $T(P)$, the firm sets its price to maximize its profit. Thus, the regulator maximizes expected welfare w.r.t. the transfer function $T(P)$:

$$\max_{T(P)} E(W) = E(V(P) + \varphi\pi(P))$$

$$s.t. \quad IC: \pi'(P^*(\theta)) = -Q(P^*(\theta))$$

$$IR: \pi(P^*(\overline{\theta})) \geq 0.$$

Here φ is the relative social weight assigned to profit. Choosing $\varphi < 1$ somewhat counters the arguments in Section 2.5 against using subsidies.

The IC is the incentive compatibility constraint, which assures that, at the equilibrium, the firm truthfully reveals its own type. In other words, the firm does not mimic any other type.

Given θ, the firm chooses its price to maximize its profit

$$\max_{p} (T(P) + PQ - \theta Q).$$

This leads to a profit-maximizing price $P^* = P^*(\theta)$.

The key idea for the IC is the following: Suppose the type θ increases by one unit, consider two cost types:

$$C_1 = \tilde{\theta} Q, C_2 = (\tilde{\theta} + 1)Q.$$

Type 1 is the low cost type, type 2 is the high cost type, the difference in cost between the two is Q.

Now suppose that, at the equilibrium, $-\frac{d\pi(P^*(\theta))}{d\theta} < Q(P^*(\theta))$, then the profit decrease in θ is less than the cost increase in θ, therefore, the *low cost type* will mimic the *high cost type*. In contrast, suppose $-\frac{d\pi(P^*(\theta))}{d\theta} > Q(P^*(\theta))$, then the profit decrease outweighs the cost increase. Therefore the *high cost type* will mimic *low cost type*.

Both are not optimal. Thus, IC requires $-\frac{d\pi(P^*(\theta))}{d\theta} = Q(P^*(\theta))$.

IR is the so-called individual rationality constraint, also known as "participation" constraint. It assures that, at the equilibrium, every type will participate. For this to hold, it is sufficient to ensure that the highest cost type will participate:

$$\pi(\bar{\theta}) \geq 0.$$

Since under a binding IR constraint the high cost type will make zero profits, all other types must make positive profits. They could always mimic the high cost type and assure themselves positive profits that way.

The IC constraint assures that they will be better off not mimicking the high cost type. Thus, the tax or subsidy must compensate for the difference in price markups between the different types.

IR and IC imply: $E(\pi(\theta)) = \int_{\underline{\theta}}^{\bar{\theta}} Q(P(\theta)) d\theta.$

Then, by *optimal control*, the constrained maximization of *E(W)* implies

$$P^*(\theta) = \theta + (1 - \alpha) \cdot \frac{F(\theta)}{f(\theta)}.$$

If $\alpha = 1$, $P^*(\theta) = \theta = MC, \forall \ \theta \in (\underline{\theta}, \bar{\theta}]$. Thus, if consumer surplus and profit are weighted equally and there is no cost of public funds, the first best optimum $P^* = MC$ is assured.

If $\alpha < 1$, $P^*(\underline{\theta}) = \underline{\theta}$, because $F(\underline{\theta}) = 0$ and $f(\underline{\theta}) > 0$. Thus, under distributional concerns, the lowest cost type will set a price equal to marginal cost and will receive a positive transfer assuring a positive profit. In contrast, if $\alpha < 1$, $P^*(\theta) > \theta$, $\forall \theta \in (\underline{\theta}, \bar{\theta}]$. Thus, all other types will set prices above marginal costs. In general, the smaller α, the larger the price markup.

Under the additional assumption that $\frac{F(\theta)}{f(\theta)}$ is monotonically increasing in θ, price and the margin above marginal cost both increase in θ. This additional assumption is known as the "increasing hazard rate" and is satisfied by most usual distributions (normal, uniform, logistic, exponential etc.). Furthermore, under this assumption, $T(P(\theta))$ decreases in θ. The regulator will give a high subsidy to low cost types to make them charge at marginal cost and give a low subsidy to high cost types but allow them to have a positive price-cost margin.

Laffont and Tirole (1986) developed a slightly more complicated model capturing the important regulatory issue of cost minimization. Their main assumption is:

the firm's cost function is $TC = C + \varphi(e) = (\theta - e)Q + \varphi(e)$.

Here e is the cost-reducing effort, which the firm chooses endogenously. It is unobservable to the regulator. The $\varphi(e)$ is the disutility to the firm (or an unobservable cost) of inducing effort. The functional form is common knowledge, known to the regulator and the firm. Furthermore, assume that $\varphi' > 0$, $\varphi'' > 0$, $\varphi(0) = 0$.

The type distribution $F(\theta)$ with $\theta \in [\underline{\theta}, \overline{\theta}]$ is also common knowledge. The regulator observes P and $MC = (\theta - e)$ and proposes the transfer based on them: $T(P, MC)$.

This is again a two-stage game. In the first stage, the regulator sets $T(P, MC)$ s.t. $p = MC$. Since MC and P are both observable, the regulator can achieve the efficient output by setting $P = MC = \theta - e$. This separates pricing from cost-reducing incentives (*incentive-pricing dichotomy*) and will leave the firm with disutility $\varphi(e)$, which can be viewed as a fixed cost that the firm chooses endogenously.

In the second stage, given $T(P)$, the firm chooses effort to maximize its profit.

Under the first-best (e is observable), the regulator's and the firm's cost minimization problem *for given Q* coincide

$$\min_e TC(Q, e) = (\theta - e)Q + \varphi(e)$$

$$F.O.C.: \quad \frac{\partial TC}{\partial e} = -Q + \varphi'(e) = 0$$

$$\Rightarrow \quad \varphi'(e^*) = Q.$$

In contrast, under the Laffont and Tirole approach, the regulator's problem is

$$\max_{T(p, MC)} E(W) = E(V(p) + \alpha\pi(p))$$

$$s.t. \quad IC: \; \pi'(\theta) = \varphi'(\theta(e^*))$$

$$IR: \; \pi\left(\overline{\theta}(e^*)\right) = 0.$$

At the solution, for $\underline{\theta}$, $\underline{e} = e^*$, e^* is first-best effort. Thus, similar to the Baron & Myerson model, the lowest cost type will behave efficiently, in this case by exerting first-best welfare-optimal effort. In contrast, for $\theta \in (\underline{\theta}, \overline{\theta}]$, $e < e^*$, which implies $\underline{MC} = \underline{\theta} - e^* < \ldots < \overline{\theta} - \overline{e} = \overline{MC}$. Again, the other cost types will behave suboptimally from a first-best perspective and exert suboptimal effort.

The subsidy T decreases in C, therefore it also decreases in θ. Since the low cost type can always mimic the high cost type, in order to induce high effort, the

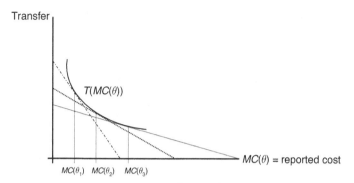

Figure 2 Convex transfer function $T\left(MC(\theta)\right)$ with linear approximations

regulator has to give this low cost type an extra bonus. This extra bonus is called the *information rent*. In addition, the information rent is decreasing in θ.

As seen in Figure 2, under the Laffont and Tirole approach, the transfer function $T(MC(\theta))$ is convex and decreases in θ. The authors suggest approximating this function by a set of linear functions so that the regulated firm can choose from a menu of such functions.

There are two main downsides of Bayesian mechanisms. The first is that Bayesian regulators cannot be monitored well by the public because the type distribution remains subjective, which makes it somewhat arbitrary (Koray & Saglam, 2005). Second, because of the complex mathematics, it is hard to gain quantitative results that are applicable to the real world.[8] However, the sophisticated approach provides strong insights into the incentive properties of regulation. For example, firms have to receive an information rent in order to be induced to "reveal" their type. In addition, the approach demonstrates that it is impossible to reach a first-best outcome. Furthermore, the approach demonstrates the large effect that regulatory commitment or the lack thereof should have on regulatory incentives. The less the regulator can commit to future policies, the weaker incentives should be. A very practical insight from many of the Bayesian models is that, because of the convexity of the optimal transfer function, the regulatory policy recommendation can be formulated as a menu of simple linear contracts. This balances the strength of incentives with the cost of the firm's rents in terms of welfare. It helps restrict the size of rents to the firm but entails some price in terms of inefficiencies in pricing and/or costs. Thus, overall, this approach is not very practical but insightful.

---

[8] Additional insights can be gained through numerical simulations with more realistic functional forms (Gasmi et al., 2002a).

3.2.2 Informationally Simple Mechanisms

Informationally simple approaches try to bridge the conflict of interest between regulator and regulated firm by finding mechanisms that change the firm's objective function in such a way that it simulates the regulator's objective function. That can either be done by tax/subsidy schemes or by imposing constraints on the firm's behavior. The simple mechanisms mostly attempt to use only observable and verifiable (bookkeeping) data and to be independent of the particular regulator.

Tax or Subsidy Mechanisms

Loeb and Magat (1979) developed the classic regulatory subsidy mechanism. The Loeb–Magat (L-M) mechanism is extremely simple. By providing the firm with a subsidy equal to the consumer surplus, the regulator can achieve the first-best outcome: In this case, the regulator and the firm share the same objective function.

The main assumptions for the implementation of L-M are that demand is common knowledge and financing a subsidy is cost free. The firm's cost is private information that only the firm knows. The firm behaves like in a competitive market, maximizing profit by charging $P = MC$. Also, the firm will minimize its cost. Thus, under the L-M assumptions, the firm will be incentivized both to set the allocatively efficient price and to minimize its cost for the resulting output. The two downsides of L-M are the information requirement on demand and the financing of the subsidy. In practice, the regulator could auction off the monopoly license and thereby recover the subsidy from the winning bidder (Sharkey, 1979). However, measuring demand is likely to be difficult and controversial. In order to solve both these problems, mechanisms derivative of L-M have been designed, the incremental surplus subsidy (ISS), in particular (Sappington & Sibley, 1988).

The ISS reduces the subsidy problem and the problem of demand measurement by providing the firm with a subsidy or taxing the firm such that its total profit equals the *change* in social surplus:

$$ISS_t = V(P_t) - V(P_{t-1}) - \pi_{t-1} \rightarrow \pi_t^{ISS} = ISS_t + \pi_t = \Delta V_t + \Delta \pi_t = \Delta W_t.$$

Sappington and Sibley assume that the firm maximizes a discounted stream of profits including the subsidy:

$$\max_{\{P_t\}_{t=1}^{\infty}} \pi^{ISS} = \sum_{t=1}^{\infty} (\Delta V_t + \Delta \pi_t) \cdot (1 + r)^{-t}.$$

Summed over all periods, the firm could earn at most $\Delta W^* = W_{max} - W_0$. Any discounting over time will make the profit less than ΔW. Therefore, the firm will make a quick adjustment to lower the price to marginal cost so that

$$P_0 > MC, \ P_1 = P_2 = \ldots = P_\infty = MC.$$

The benefits of the ISS are, in particular, immediate optimal pricing and investment by the firm, which will earn no rents after the first period. The downsides include imperfect cost-reducing incentives (Blackmon, 1992) and the remaining question how to measure the change in consumer surplus.

Price Cap Mechanisms

The best known of the constraint-based mechanisms are price caps. They have been applied to telecommunications pricing worldwide but, with the exception of the UK, less in other network industries. Their success comes from combining two characteristics that are essential for regulation today, (a) incentives for cost reductions and (b) freedom and incentives for price rebalancing.

The key idea here is to allow the firm to freely set its prices, as long as they obey a price-cap formula. In order to allow for a multiproduct context, the prices are combined in a price index formed by the basket of regulated services. This price index for the current period is constrained ("capped") by last period's index adjusted by several factors, which usually include an inflation factor and a so-called X factor. Thus,

$$\frac{\sum_{i=1}^{n} P_i^t Q_i^{t-1}}{\sum_{i=1}^{n} P_i^{t-1} Q_i^{t-1}} \leq 1 + I - X.$$

Here I measures inflation as a percentage markup and X represents envisaged productivity increases. Since I already captures the national productivity increase across all sectors, X only captures the productivity increase above the average level in the economy. The original price-cap proposal by Littlechild (1983) set $I = \Delta RPI$, which is the change in the British consumer price index. This inflation measure captures the consumer side. Input price inflation faced by the firm may be higher or lower than this. The inflation and the X factor together are meant to fulfill two functions.

First, they should trace the firm's costs reasonably well so that the firm over time neither makes undesirably high profits nor suffers losses. This should establish results that are fair to the firm and its consumers and it should therefore increase the regulator's ability to commit for a longer period (Vogelsang, 2006).

Second, these factors should not be influenced by the firm's actual behavior so that the firm has strong incentives to minimize its costs. If it reduces (increases) its costs, its profit would increase (decrease) by the full cost reduction (increase). This property would provide for productive efficiency.

A third desirable property of Littlechild's price caps is that the firm can readjust its price structure within the price index. Littlechild uses a Laspeyres price index always with last period's quantities as weights. As shown by Vogelsang and Finsinger (1979) a price cap based on a Laspeyres index has the tendency over time to converge toward the Ramsey price structure.

Thus, the Littlechild formula, in principle, has several properties compatible with welfare maximization. In practice, however, both costs and demands change so that full convergence will not be achieved and profits will deviate from the desired goal. As a result, the price cap formula needs to be adjusted every few years. In practice, this updating has either been done via firm-based planning models, such as in the UK, or based on rate-of-return regulation criteria, such as in most other countries.

This last practice has led to questions if price caps are really different from rate-of-return regulation (Liston, 1993; Vogelsang, 2006). However, there are distinct differences between the two approaches. In particular, within the limits set by the price index formula, price caps give the regulated firms discretion over individual prices. In contrast, there is usually no pricing discretion under rate-of-return regulation. Furthermore, there is usually a predetermined long regulatory lag under price caps, whereas the lag under rate-of-return regulation is endogenously determined by the achieved rate of return. Last, there is a full cost pass-through under rate-of-return regulation, while the pass-through under price caps every few years is uncertain. The uncertainty can be reduced by the use of further adjustment factors "Y" or "Z" for tax changes and/or specific input price adjustments.

Overall, the cost-reducing and price-setting incentives provided by price caps have been softer than the theoretical ideal, largely because of the adjustments of the formula over time. If the adjustments are done in a predictable way based on rate-of-return criteria, they soften the incentives because they are based on the firm's actual costs including any inefficiencies. This means that cost-reducing incentives tend to be strongest right after such an adjustment and weakest right before (Vogelsang, 1989a). If the adjustment is based on other criteria, similar effects can be expected because regulators typically cannot commit beforehand on the method used for such an adjustment, thereby creating a ratcheting problem. Some countries, such as New Zealand, have increased commitment by prescribing "input methodologies" for all regulated network industries that can only be adjusted in long time intervals.

Thus, the performance of price caps is strongly influenced by the skills and commitment of the regulator and generally ranks between that of rate-of-return regulation and that of an ideal price cap system.

Two-part Tariff Mechanisms

Both subsidy mechanisms and simple constraint-based mechanisms can be converted into constraint-based two-part tariffs. Subsidy mechanisms can thereby lose the subsidy requirement and become more applicable (Laffont & Tirole, 1993), while simple constraint-based mechanisms can become more efficient (Vogelsang, 1989b). Under fairly general assumptions for every linear price, there exists a Pareto superior two-part tariff (Willig, 1978). Nevertheless, two-part tariffs have some drawbacks. In particular, they can exclude customers and act like a regressive tax (Florio, 2013). If applied to firms as buyers, they can also interfere with competition (Hoernig & Vogelsang, 2013).

Hesamzadeh et al. (2018) have recently proposed a mechanism merging the price cap approach with the subsidy mechanism ISS. It is called HRGV after its four authors. It consists of a multiproduct two-part tariff for an electricity transmission company (Transco), where the variable fees are given by the congestion charges, and the fixed fee is constrained by last period's fixed fee plus this period's change in consumer surplus.[9] Thus, under HRGV, the individual user's fixed fee f_t in period t is constrained by

$$f_t \leq f_{t-1} + (V_t - V_{t-1})/N.$$

Here N is the number of users. The consumer surplus here is the surplus from transmission services and therefore equals the sum of generator surplus and load surplus. This approach is quite similar to but nevertheless differs from the ISS by using no subsidies, by including cumulative consumer surplus changes and by not deducting profits. Although it uses a dynamic setting, it is thereby closer to L-M than to the ISS. HRGV has several good welfare properties in that it incentivizes the firm always to invest in such a way that the resulting capacities and congestion charges are efficient and that it provides the firm with strong cost minimizing incentives. Its main drawback is that the Transco may make very high profits. A further drawback is that congestion charges have to be calculated by the regulatory agency or by an independent system operator (ISO). While this is very feasible, it may be difficult to get similar information in other network industries. Other than that, the mechanism can easily be adapted to other network industries by replacing the congestion charges by variable prices for all the outputs sold by a network.

Vogelsang (2018a and 2020) has extensively discussed ways for a practical application of this theoretically attractive mechanism to electricity transmission networks. For that purpose, several adjustments should be made. These

---

[9] Because of economies of scale, efficient congestion charges in an optimally built network will not be cost covering. Thus, a fixed fee is necessary to compensate.

adjustments and their motivation illustrate the general problems encountered in translating theoretical mechanisms into practical applications, something I have experienced ever since proposing my first regulatory incentive schemes in the late 1970s. In the case of HRGV, the buyers of electricity transmission services are electricity generators and loads.[10] Their demands for transmission services can only be used directly for calculating "consumer surplus" if they behave competitively. Otherwise the mechanism's working may be distorted, although it will still have attractive properties (Vogelsang, 2020). More severe is that

(a) by receiving all the additional surplus generated by its investments, the Transco may make high profits that could be viewed as unfair by regulators and users and

(b) the contribution of other players, such as electricity generators in jointly creating the additional surplus, may be hard to distinguish and to reward (unless the Transco does that voluntarily).

The fairness issue (a) can be dealt with in three ways. First, there can be an "I-X" type adjustment made like the one discussed previously for price caps. This will lead to some distortion, which will be minor if X is small. One can avoid this by using an additive rather than a multiplicative I-X adjustment (Vogelsang, 2018a). The second possibility is to use profit sharing for users by reducing their fixed fees by their profit share. This will not distort investment and variable pricing but may reduce cost-reducing incentives. The third possibility is to use a Bayesian menu approach, which requires assessing some type distribution $F(\theta)$.

Conclusions on Simple Mechanisms

While simple mechanisms lack the optimality properties of Bayesian mechanisms, they have proven to be useful and influential. In particular, they utilize the regulated firm's informational advantage by (a) somewhat aligning the firm's and the regulator's objectives and (b) giving the firm some discretion to improve both profits and welfare. They are therefore based on the same insight as the Bayesian schemes that firms have to be able to command some rents as a price for using the information advantage to benefit the public. Simple mechanisms, in practice, achieve good results with a limited set of instruments, such as two-part tariffs.

---

[10] Since generators may compete with each other while loads generally do not, it may be preferable to have loads as buyers. This would avoid the anticompetitive effects of two-part tariffs described in Hoernig and Vogelsang (2013).

4 The Emergence of Competition and Its Effect on Regulation

4.1 The Issues

In recent decades, competition has entered many network industries. This new development was associated with several other related issues. First, regulatory reform happened both independent of and as a response to the emergence of competition. The second related issue is privatization, which means the sale of state-owned network companies to private shareholders. This also was associated with regulatory reform and with the advent of competition. Although privatization is often viewed as a prerequisite for meaningful competition, the example of China shows that state-owned mobile telephone networks can actually compete with each other.[11] The third concept is liberalization, which means that competition is allowed. This has been an important step in network industries, which hitherto had been perceived as natural monopolies, where competition would be deemed inefficient. Liberalization represents the view that either natural monopolies no longer persist or that competition can improve on the regulation of natural monopolies.

The last relevant concept is that of deregulation. It means that the state gives up regulation. This will in general occur only if competition is viewed strong enough to replace regulation. Also, from a policy perspective, no vacuum is created because competition policy is typically applied to all industries and in particular to those that were previously regulated.

4.2 Policy Options for Liberalization

Traditionally, entry by competitors was not allowed in regulated public-utility industries. Two features were mentioned as dangers of entry. First, duplication of networks in natural monopoly settings would be wasteful, and, second, competition would be destructive in the sense that no firms could survive and continue to invest. On the other hand, the natural monopoly property is (a) hard to prove empirically and (b) may no longer hold as markets grow and technologies change. A third and important feature relevant for disallowing entry was that entry would interfere with regulatory policies, such as deliberate cross subsidization. As a result, those policies either had to be changed or entry had to be handicapped. This came out particularly strongly in telecommunications, where local calling charges were traditionally subsidized by long-distance

---

[11] While privatization was a prime policy issue in the 1980s and 1990s, a new interest in state-owned enterprises has meanwhile emerged that triggered an interesting new literature. This is, among others, associated with the success of Chinese public enterprises in telecommunications markets. See, for example, Musacchio and Lazzarini (2014) and the momentous work of Bernier et al. (2020).

charges but where market entry was economical first for long-distance services. Thus, both the technical developments and the overpriced long-distance services created the desire for entry by new suppliers and their potential customers. Here incumbents were successful in preventing entry for some time and thereafter entry was handicapped by high wholesale access charges for the local services that entrants needed in order to offer the long-distance services.

The question is, what errors occur if one permits or disallows entry? The error in allowing entry would be that the market really is a natural monopoly and regulation is efficient enough so that the market outcome under monopoly would be better than under free entry. The latter includes that either entry actually occurs or, if not, that the entry threat is strong enough to induce more efficient behavior of the monopolist than regulation. The error in forbidding entry would be that the market is not a natural monopoly so that competition would lead to lower costs or that, even if it were a natural monopoly, there would be enough efficiency-enhancing competition to overcome the drawbacks of regulation and the cost of duplication. For the purpose of clarifying the errors involved, Vogelsang (2002) has differentiated between weak and strong natural monopolies, where strong natural monopoly means that the cost advantages of monopoly and the costs of duplication are large, while under weak natural monopoly the advantages of monopoly on costs of duplication are small.

In the absence of good measurements of the natural monopoly property, allowing entry while imposing price caps on the incumbent can be a good policy with little downside risk. One of the main goals pursued with the introduction of price caps was to accommodate competition. It was the advance of competition that had made rate-of-return regulation obsolete and that, in the 1980s, induced the FCC and the British government to look for alternative ways of utility regulation. Price-cap regulation keeps the incumbent's prices at fairly efficient levels with a fairly efficient structure. My conjecture is that such pricing would eliminate the dangers from opening the market because the prices, in case of a strong natural monopoly, would already be so low that an entrant could not break even. Under price-cap regulation with some form of commitment, entrants would expect that prices could not afterward increase to entry. As a result, with strong natural monopoly, entrants could not hope for the incumbent to increase prices to recover the cost increase from entry (this would take the form of thinning out the subscriber base of a network).[12] In contrast, under rate-of-return regulation, prices could be increased, provided demands are

---

[12] Evans and Guthrie (2012) show that this argument may not hold under lumpy investment, which requires high prices shortly before new capacity investments. Regular price caps would not allow that, although price caps with a basket of differently dated services might.

sufficiently inelastic. If, in the presence of price caps, competition occurs and spreads out quickly, we may suspect the absence of natural monopoly or the presence of only weak natural monopoly.

Allowing competition does not necessarily mean that free entry is allowed. For example, in the 1980s, the then UK Office of Telecommunications (Oftel) allowed only one entrant (Mercury) to compete with the incumbent British Telecom. This was based on the idea that there were strong economies of scale and sunk costs that would prevent a company from entering if there was the fear of another entrant. This policy proved to be unsuccessful and was later revoked. A problem here is that the market under free entry helps solve the selection problem so that the most efficient firms are the most likely entrants. Almost worldwide entry restrictions are still imposed in mobile telephony, where firms compete in auctions for a limited number of spectrum licenses, usually three or four. In most other network markets, entry is no longer legally restricted.

Opening former monopoly markets to competition has raised the question if regulation can be abandoned at the same time. Such immediate deregulation has been exceedingly rare. Rather, at least the former monopolist continues to be regulated for some time, while the new entrants are often free of regulation. Such asymmetric regulation addresses two issues. The first is to shield end users from exploitation by the continuing market power of the incumbent. This motivation loses justification as competition improves. The second issue is that potential entrants have to overcome severe entry barriers in the form of essential facilities (bottlenecks) that they need as inputs to enter the market but that are controlled by the incumbent. Thus, access to such essential facilities may need to be regulated. Such regulation is hampered by conflicts of interest of the incumbent between supplying such access to competitors and selling directly to end users.

4.3 Vertical Integration vs. Separation

Both this conflict of interest and the remaining market power of incumbents vis-à-vis end users have led to drastic policy solutions in some countries and some industries in the form of vertical and/or horizontal split up of incumbent firms. So far, we have concentrated on regulation of firm behavior/conduct. Now we add regulation of the vertical and possibly the horizontal structure of the regulated firm. For example, the vertically integrated electric utilities in the European Union have been forced to vertically separate their transmission and distribution networks from their generation and sales activities. The tradeoff here is between solving the conflict of interest and losing economies of scope between the vertical stages of production. Horizontal separation has been rarer, because it is hard to do within a geographic area. For example, the separation of electric utilities in Argentina into two regional companies was not really horizontal separation, because the two resulting companies did not compete with each other.

The choice of structural regulation depends on the effectiveness of conduct regulation and on the efficiencies of vertical and/or horizontal integration. Borrowing from the *theory of the firm*, we here concentrate on vertical efficiencies. If vertical efficiencies outweigh the effects of anticompetitive behavior, vertical integration is in order. Otherwise vertical separation may be justified.

Vertical integration means that transactions between different stages of production are carried out within the firm rather than in markets between firms. Vertical integration is preferred over market transactions if the internal "transactions costs" are lower than those incurred in a market. The use of transactions costs as the explanatory variable for the existence of firms (and hence for vertical integration) goes back to Coase (1937) and has been extended by Williamson (1975, 1979). Typically, when there are many buyers and sellers in the market, no problem of transaction costs arises. Similarly, under monopoly with many buyers, transaction costs tend to be low. It is the case of few parties or even only one party on both sides of a potential market, where transaction costs tend to become a problem. The extreme case would be that of a bilateral monopoly consisting of a monopolistic seller and a monopsonistic buyer.

Such situations arise, in particular, for so-called specific assets on both sides of the market. The investment in such assets is often relation specific, meaning that both sides make investments in view of their upcoming or ongoing relationship. Such investments often save a lot of money relative to general investments that continue to be open to other parties on both sides. A classic example for such a situation of relation-specific investments is that of coal mines and power plants in areas such as the Appalachian mountains in the eastern USA. In this case, converting coal into electricity at the mine and transporting the electricity from the coal mines to the cities is cheaper than transporting coal to the cities and converting it to electricity there. Thus, those "mine-mouth plants" are the cost-efficient solution. Also, optimally sized coal mines and power plants match quite well so that one mine feeds one plant. Ex ante, there are potentially many sites for coal mines and power plants so that there is potential choice and potential competition on both sides. However, after a choice of site has been made, contracts for up to forty to forty-five years have been signed, and investments have been sunk, the situation becomes one of bilateral monopoly. It is unlikely that the mine has other potential customers conveniently located or that the power plant can easily get coal from elsewhere. This change from ex ante bilateral competition to ex post bilateral monopoly has been called the "fundamental transformation" (Williamson, 1979). Specific assets generally involve sunk costs. As a result, leaving the relationship means giving up such sunk costs.

In principle, the transaction cost problem from the fundamental transformation can be solved through the market via a long-term contract, as it is often done in the aforementioned mine-mouth example. However, due to unforeseen contingencies, such contracts tend to be incomplete. Thus, renegotiation is often needed, which (due to the so-called hold-up problem) usually hurts one of the parties. My own personal experience in international coal trade has been that, during the 1973 oil crisis, price stipulations in international long-term coal contracts were no longer honored by suppliers who demanded renegotiations with quantity reductions and price increases. Buyers had to give in because of lack of alternative energy sources for electricity generation. Thus, although buyers might have won damages in court, that would not have solved their short-term supply problems.

How would vertical integration solve the hold-up problem? Under vertical integration, both relation-specific assets are under common ownership, meaning that the owner has the wide property rights associated with ownership. This does not mean absolute control, since the owner still depends on the cooperation of others, such as employees and other input suppliers. These relationships may be subject to other hold-up problems but not necessarily so. The owner of the vertically integrated firm has "residual" rights for all cases not specified by "contractual" rights, thereby leaving no undefined rights in case of unforeseen contingencies.

Other reasons for or against vertical integration besides relation-specific assets include risk sharing and externalities. Both markets and firms can provide tools for reducing risks. By integration, firms can ensure necessary supplies, when markets would become tight. In contrast, markets can provide insurance through diversification and risk pooling. Thus, the advantages of markets versus vertical integration depend on the types of risk.

If there are positive or negative externalities between different stages of production, vertical integration can lead to their internalization or elimination. Such externalities can, however, also be dealt with through negotiation (Coase theorem) or through government policies, although both of these involve serious coordination problems.

A very real transaction-cost problem relevant for network industries involves so-called double marginalization. It results from successive market power on two stages of production, the extreme case being successive monopolies. In contrast to a bilateral monopoly, where a single seller faces a single buyer, under successive monopoly a single seller faces a buyer, who is also a single seller in its downstream market. Bilateral monopoly and successive monopoly can occur together but need not. For example, a monopoly electricity transmission company may face many electricity distribution companies that are themselves monopolistic sellers to end users.

In successive monopolies, the upstream seller sells to the downstream seller with a price markup on marginal costs and the downstream seller sells to end users with a markup on its marginal costs, which already include the upstream markup. This double markup creates an inefficiency that can be resolved through vertical integration, which would in this case lead to a win-win situation both in the form of higher profit for the combined firm than the sum of profits for the separate firms and for the end users, who receive a lower price with only one monopoly markup. In principle, double marginalization can also be avoided through nonlinear pricing of the upstream product, but this would be associated with severe coordination problems.

Why then are not all transactions done within firms rather than through markets? Firms in particular involve personal relationships, which are guided by employment contracts that need monitoring and incentives for achieving efficient outcomes. Such incentives are usually much stronger in markets than within firms. In markets, a customer will easily "dismiss" a supplier, who does not deliver the goods in the desired quality at the desired price. In contrast, because of personal long-term relationships, punishment for failure in firms is usually softer.

Furthermore, under vertical integration, some specialization advantages available on a horizontal stage (economies of scale) may not be available, because the integrated firm would have to expand all stages of production to be able to make use of these specialization advantages. This can lead to diseconomies of scale on some of these other stages.

Summing up the discussion so far, the upsides of vertical integration include a solution to the holdup problem and to coordination problems between stages of production, while the downsides include potentially softer incentives than in market relationships and potential loss of horizontal specialization advantages. In addition, the potentially anticompetitive effects of vertical integration include, in particular, the foreclosure of an essential input and rising of rivals' costs. Foreclosure means that the incumbent firm either does not sell the essential input at all or sells it at a high price relative to the price of the downstream service that is produced with the essential input.

Foreclosure is not always profitable for the vertically integrated firm. For example, if a downstream competitor offers a differentiated product or has a better sales strategy than the incumbent, keeping the downstream competitor alive and healthy may be profitable for the incumbent. Generally there is little incentive for foreclosure if there are fixed proportions between the essential input and the downstream output and if there is perfect competition downstream. In this case, the upstream firm can already reap all monopoly profits from the upstream sale (Chicago school argument). Also, the downstream firms may be more efficient downstream than the upstream firm. However, if there are variable proportions between the facility in question and other inputs, the vertically integrated incumbent may want to foreclose downstream rivals in order to eliminate the possibility of the downstream firm substituting away from the essential input. This may, however, not always be successful if substitution by the downstream firm is sufficiently easy. Rather, the incentive to foreclose may be greatest, when substitution is hard but not impossible. Furthermore, the integrated incumbent will have strong foreclosure incentives if the downstream market is characterized by market power. In that case, foreclosure can eliminate double marginalization and in that sense can be efficient.

No doubt the modern developments of information and communications technology (ICT) have a major influence on the transaction costs of using markets or firm-internal transactions. In general, ICT has lowered communication and information costs substantially. However, this holds both for the costs of internal transactions and for costs of using markets. Thus, the influence of ICT on the relative costs of the two institutional arrangements is hard to disentangle. Furthermore, ICT has not only reduced the costs for vertical relationships but also for horizontal transactions. Again, the effects are ambiguous. On the one hand, ICT has increased the geographic market sizes, allowing economies of scale to be exhausted or allowing for duplication without excessive costs. On the other hand, ICT allows small firms to become more efficient, thus allowing for economies of scale to become less important for the industries affected. Again, the overall effect can be ambiguous. For example, access to the Cloud can provide small firms with access to powerful computing, data etc. At the same time the Cloud itself is characterized by strong economies of scale. Very important is also that ICT, by creating network effects, may favor endogenous sunk costs to be established at a global level, thereby favoring economies of scale that are not exhaustible (Sutton, 1991). Because of these ambiguities, the effects of ICT on network structures becomes an empirical question.

An important example of the influence of ICT on vertical relationships in networks is the emergence of over-the-top-services (OTT) on the Internet. These services are generally provided over the networks of Internet service providers (ISPs) but, at the same time, they often provide services that compete with downstream services of the vertically integrated ISPs. A case in point is

Skype, which competes with telephone sby ISPs. This leads to interesting new competitive situations somewhat similar to those we discuss in Section 4.5 as wholesale access problems.

4.4 The Network Access Problem

The regulatory requirement of bottleneck access or essential facility access builds on an antitrust policy requirement known as the "essential facilities doctrine" going back to the 1912 Terminal Railroads case.[13] An essential facility under the antitrust doctrine has the following five properties:

1. It is owned by a single party.
2. It is difficult or impossible for others to duplicate (natural monopoly property in association with sunk costs).
3. It is essential for competitors to compete (no easy substitution by other inputs).
4. The incumbent owner does not allow the access of entrants.
5. The incumbent could provide access to entrants without excessive difficulty.

Property 3 assures that, in principle, a relevant market for an essential facility can be determined. Forcing the owner of an essential facility to provide access to it runs into several problems under competition policy, because it involves setting a price, updating the price over time and setting and monitoring conditions and quality of service – all activities that competition policy agencies have not been designed for. The essential facilities doctrine has therefore not had a very successful antitrust history but rather has caught on as the basis for industry-specific regulation of wholesale access to an incumbent's bottleneck facilities.

Compared to end-user regulation, the regulation of access to an intermediate input is much more complex. This holds for several reasons. First, the intermediate input is usually a complicated product that in many cases incumbents would not offer at all without regulation. Thus, the regulator typically first has to define the product and how entrants can access it. Second, the input supplier may or may not be vertically integrated. Vertical separation simplifies regulation but may sacrifice vertical efficiencies. In contrast, vertical integration creates a conflict of interest for the incumbent between being an input supplier and a downstream competitor. Third, the input demand and the welfare effects are influenced by the fact that the downstream firms imperfectly compete with each other and may or may not be able to bypass the input. Fourth, bottleneck access regulation may interact with end-user regulation, which may or may not have to be abandoned. Last, bottleneck access regulation involves downstream

---

[13] UNITED STATES v. TERMINAL R.R. ASS'N, 224 U.S. 383 (1912).

entrants as an additional interest group besides end users and incumbents. They all will try to influence regulators in a political economy game (Briglauer et al., 2019).

4.5 Types of Wholesale Access Regulation

4.5.1 Access Pricing under Vertical Separation vs. Integration

Wholesale access pricing under vertical separation is conceptually simpler than under vertical integration, because it poses only a straightforward market power problem and not a conflict of interest problem. In this case, the conventional Ramsey pricing formula may apply. This will hold (1) if the derived demand for the intermediate input directly translates into the final good demand, (2) if competition downstream is perfect and (3) if there are fixed proportions between the intermediate input and the final output. If the downstream firm has market power in the end-user market, it will charge a price there with a markup over its marginal cost and that will create a double markup given the markup for the intermediate input. Thus, Ramsey pricing in this case will be associated with double marginalization, which increases inefficiency. This may be healed if, in addition to market power, there is free entry downstream. In this case, increasing the markup for the wholesale product may prevent excessive entry, thus counteracting the negative effect of double marginalization.[14]

Under vertical integration of the incumbent, the wholesale access seekers are both the incumbent's customers upstream and competitors downstream. The resulting conflict of interest can induce the incumbent to attempt foreclosing the access seekers and to do so by trying to undermine regulated wholesale access. In particular, forcing the incumbent to sell the wholesale access product at a low price would create incentives to deteriorate the quality of access. This is a common problem of wholesale access regulation, known as "sabotage." Fully solving this problem of lower quality requires a sufficiently high wholesale access price (Bose et al., 2017).

4.5.2 The Efficient Component Pricing Rule (ECPR)

A pricing approach that specifically deals with the conflict of interest is the "efficient component pricing rule" (ECPR), first developed by Baumol (1983). The key idea here is to set the regulated wholesale access price in such a way that the incumbent is indifferent between selling the wholesale input to

---

[14] If competition in the market is not fierce and if the market is profitable, excessive entry can be expected in the sense that there is too much cost duplication relative to the efficiency gains from price reduction. See, for example, Mankiw and Whinston (1986) on excessive entry under Cournot competition.

competitors and selling the downstream output to end users. Thus, the wholesale access price has to cover the cost of wholesale access plus the profit contribution downstream that would be lost by selling the wholesale product and thereby losing sales of the end-user product. Baumol calls this loss of profit contribution the "opportunity cost" of selling access. I use quotes here, because this is not necessarily an opportunity cost in welfare terms but rather only a private opportunity cost. In the simplest case, where the sale of each unit of access upstream leads to the loss of one unit of sales downstream, this leads to the so-called margin rule, under which the ECPR access price equals the end-user price minus the unit cost downstream. Thus, the access price a becomes

$$a = C_a + private \; opportunity \; cost = P_{enduser} - unit \; cost \; downstream.$$

Here C_a is the marginal cost of access.

The ECPR has nice economic properties if the incumbent's downstream price is efficiently regulated. In that case, downstream firms will only enter if their downstream costs are lower than those of the incumbent. This assures efficient entry. However, the rule has been highly controversial for the case that downstream prices are not regulated. In that case, provided the incumbent enjoys market power, he or she can increase the downstream price to the monopoly level and will automatically receive a similar increase in the access price. Thus, the access price does not really restrict the market power of the incumbent. Such restriction would require alternative competition downstream, for example, by a different technology. Even without such competition, the ECPR will protect downstream entrants from a price squeeze (foreclosure). Entrants may also introduce some product differentiation within the limits set by the use of the incumbent's wholesale input.

4.5.3 "Global" Ramsey Pricing

So far, we have considered Ramsey pricing only for the case of end-user prices. In principle, the Ramsey pricing approach of constrained welfare maximization can also be applied to the combination of wholesale access and the incumbent's downstream products. This is highly complex, but the major insights can already be provided in a simple example by Laffont and Tirole (2000, box 3.1) for the case of local and long-distance telephone calls.[15] The main assumptions are:

1. The essential input, local access, is produced with economies of scale by the incumbent.
2. Long-distance calling is produced at constant returns to scale but at different costs by incumbent and by potential entrants.

---

[15] For a similar derivation, see Armstrong and Sappington (2007, equation 109).

3. In addition, long-distance calling requires the essential input, which is provided for an access charge a.
4. Local calling is the incumbent's monopoly with demand independent from that of long-distance calling.
5. Long-distance calling is provided by the incumbent and the entrants.
6. Entrants provide homogeneous long-distance services in Bertrand competition with each other. Thus, their profits vanish.
7. The incumbent's long-distance service is differentiated from that of the entrants.
8. Welfare is maximized with regard to the incumbent's prices for local and long-distance calling and the entrants' price for long-distance calling and is subject to a break-even constraint of the incumbent. Note that the access charge a does not appear here, because it is defined by the entrants' long-distance price and their zero-profit condition.

Thus, the incumbent's profit is:

$$\pi_1 \ (P_0, P_1, P_2) = (P_0 - 2c_0)Q_0 + (P_1 - c_1 - 2c_0)Q_1 + (a - 2c_0)Q_2.$$

This profit consists of three parts:

$(P_0 - 2c_0)Q_0$ is local service profit. Note that local access needs to be provided twice (i.e., for call origination and termination).
$(P_1 - c_1 - 2c_0)Q_1$ is long-distance profit.
$(a - 2c_0)Q_2 = (P_2 - c_2 - 2c_0)Q_2$ is the profit from selling access to the entrants

The regulator maximizes welfare in the local and long-distance market:

$$\max_{p0, p1, p2} \ W = [V(P_0) + V(P_1, P_2) + \pi_1 \ (P_0, P_1, P_2)]$$

$$s.t. \quad P_{i, \ i=0,1,2} \geq 0.$$

The usual Ramsey pricing conditions involve the direct elasticity for local calls and the super elasticities for long-distance calling. They allow solving for the access charge, which becomes:

$$\Rightarrow \ a = 2c_0 + \delta(P_1 - c_1 - 2 \ c_0) + \frac{\lambda}{1+\lambda} \cdot \frac{P_2}{\varepsilon_2}.$$

Here $2c_0 = $ marginal cost of local access (both sides),
$c_1 = $ marginal cost of adding long distance by incumbent,
$P_1 = $ long distance price by incumbent,
$P_2 = $ long distance price by entrants,
$\varepsilon_2 = $ direct long distance demand elasticity faced by entrants

The last composite expression is a Ramsey markup related to entrants' end-user demand, while the expression in parentheses is the incumbent's long-distance markup on the incumbent's marginal cost of long-distance services. The term δ is known as the displacement ratio or business-stealing effect,

$$\delta = \frac{\partial Q_1/\partial P_2}{\partial Q_2/\partial P_2}.$$

It expresses how much the incumbent loses in downstream long-distance sales relative to its gain in wholesale access sales in response to a price reduction by the entrants. If the incumbent's and entrants' long-distance services are imperfect substitutes, $\delta < 1$. Thus, overall, the Ramsey access charge will be the marginal cost of access plus an ECPR-type markup multiplied by the diversion ratio plus a Ramsey markup to cover the incumbent's costs due to economies of scale.

4.5.4 Sophisticated ECPR

Armstrong, Doyle and Vickers (ADV, 1996) have developed a sophisticated version of the ECPR that reflects Baumol's original intention better than the margin rule and is closely related to the Ramsey access pricing rule just described. Under idealized conditions, the clean margin rule makes the incumbent indifferent between selling upstream or downstream. These conditions include (i) fixed technical proportions between the access product and the downstream product, (ii) competitive pricing downstream and (iii) homogeneity of the downstream product.

The approach by ADV addresses factors that violate these conditions and are likely to hold and be relevant in reality. They include, in particular, that the downstream outputs may be differentiated between those of the regulated firm and those of the access seekers and that therefore downstream competition will be imperfect. ADV also consider the possibility of bypass of the regulated firm's access and of technical substitution. In these cases, the ECPR price is derived by multiplying the downstream margin that is added to the direct (or marginal) cost of access by the displacement ratio δ (or business stealing effect). Thus,

$$a = 2c_0 + \delta(P_1 - c_1 - 2\,c_0).$$

Under the conditions of the clean margin rule, we have by assumption $\delta = 1$. However, under product differentiation downstream, one gets $\delta < 1$. In fact, in the ADV model, the displacement ratio is the product of the separate displacement effects of product differentiation (δ_d), bypass (δ_b) and technological substitutability (δ_t): $\delta = \delta_d \cdot \delta_b \cdot \delta_t$. Since each of these components is smaller than 1, the total effect can reduce the ECPR markup substantially.

While this sophisticated ECPR is a little simpler than Ramsey pricing, it has, to the best of my knowledge, never been used in practice. However, regulators all over the world have achieved a similar result by twisting the margin rule in favor of entrants. In particular, they typically do not use the incumbent's actual costs saved but rather the incumbent's costs of expansion or even a reasonably efficient entrant's cost of expansion. These cost concepts differ by the sunk costs incurred downstream by the incumbent and by scale differences between the incumbent and a reasonably efficient entrant.

4.5.5 Cost-Based Access Pricing

All pricing rules discussed so far are either inadequate in containing market power (margin rule) or too complicated to apply (Ramsey pricing or sophisticated ECPR). In practice, therefore, cost-based pricing has dominated under bottleneck access regulation.[16] In contrast to traditional rate-of-return regulation, cost-based pricing in many countries now uses efficient cost as the pricing base. The question is, what does one mean by efficient cost?

Modeling Efficient Cost

Such costs are determined by the regulator, either based on costs reported by the regulated firm and then adjusted for alleged inefficiencies or based on a cost model. Australia and New Zealand, for example, use a building block model with a somewhat similar structure as US rate-of-return regulation but with efficiency adjustments. The main cost concept applied in cost models has been LRIC (long-run incremental cost). Generally, in the long run, a firm has enough flexibility in its input decisions to make adjustments such that it will produce at its lowest cost, which can be used as efficient cost. Usually LRIC is averaged over the whole access service (LRAIC).

Where does the regulator get the information to measure costs? First of all, accounting data provide bookkeeping costs of all inputs. For this purpose, regulators usually require firms to provide specific regulatory accounts. Second, the regulator will engage specialists, such as engineers, to provide engineering data that form relationships between inputs and outputs. Under a technical point of view, through what technical processes will inputs transform into outputs? Third, the regulator has to use statistical data to build relationships between time-series and/or cross-sectional accounting data on inputs and outputs, based on which one can assign different costs to different products.

Two principal approaches, top-down and bottom-up, are used for cost calculations. Under the top-down approach, cost measurements start from the cost

---

[16] Spulber and Yoo (2009) make the case that it is impossible to calculate the cost of using a telecommunications network, because there are always systemic effects from using the network. Essentially, they make an externality argument that any call between two points has effects on the whole network. This argument bears similarity with the loop-flow effects in electricity transmission.

data provided by the firm, which usually is not publicly accessible. This issue of confidentiality generates limitations for cost measurements. Furthermore, one has to find statistical relationships between accounting costs and output-related variables in order to extrapolate from current output levels to those under regulation. Finally, there is the need to detect inefficiencies.

In contrast, the bottom-up approach starts by constructing costs from an engineering point of view of building and running the network. Since the engineer's blueprints tend to be overly optimistic, they may underestimate costs. Overall, it is usually better to use the bottom-up method for network building while using top-down methods for network operation.[17]

Cost models using the LRIC or LRAIC concepts use forward-looking costs. The idea behind this is that both the incumbent and entrants would make efficient investments and use efficient costs based on their expectation of the future. If their expectations are fulfilled, the firm will be neither overcompensated (over-invest) nor under-compensated (under-invest). However, if the costs of inputs are increasing over time and if access prices are adjusted accordingly, then the forward-looking method will lead to overcompensation. Otherwise, if the cost of inputs is decreasing over time, the forward-looking method will lead to under-compensation, and therefore the firm will prefer using the historic method.

Historic costing allows the firm, over time, to recover all the costs incurred initially. This makes historic cost pricing equitable. In contrast, if current and historic costs deviate from each other, historic costing has no good efficiency properties. However, if historic costs are always depreciated using economic depreciation, the current costs and historic costs coincide under many circumstances (Rogerson, 2011). The two methods are equivalent in theory and require very similar types of information. In particular, calculating the value today of an asset that was purchased last period either requires knowing the cost of building that asset today, or knowing what the market price of such asset would be today. Rogerson (in private communication) gives preference to historic costing, because it carries more commitment for the regulator not to expropriate the firm. If the asset is no longer produced but rather replaced by a different (equivalent) asset, both methods of valuation fail. We deal with this issue later in this section.

Cost-based pricing faces the problem of common cost assignment discussed previously for rate-of-return regulation. Common costs need to be assigned to services in order to allow the incumbent to break even. However, there exists no clean assignment method. This is less problematic if the direct costs of each service are measured correctly, because then there will only be a small amount

---

[17] Gasmi et al. (2002b) determine natural monopoly by simulating an engineering model.

of common costs to be assigned. In telecommunications networks, this is normally about 8–10 percent. Even the remaining "common costs" will contain costs that are directly incurred by individual services but are hard to measure. They will usually be fairly proportional to the amount of the service produced. For both these reasons, proportional markups are used in practice.

Too Little Investment: Reversal of Averch–Johnson

To the extent that regulators determine costs from models, there is little danger of an Averch–Johnson effect. On the contrary, firms often claim that they are not sufficiently rewarded for risk-taking, leaving them with insufficient incentives to invest. A very major critique of the model-based approach is that the resulting access prices do not reflect uncertainty, dynamics and imperfections in the building of the bottleneck assets and therefore that LRIC severely underestimates the actual costs of incumbents and does not reward them for their risk-taking. In particular, since the bottleneck's costs are largely sunk, the access seekers receive a free option, because the incumbents assume the investment risks ex ante, while the access seekers only buy access ex post, when much of the uncertainty is revealed. Major critics of the LRIC approach (called TELRIC in the USA), such as Hausman (1997) and Pindyck (2007), have therefore used theoretical models to calculate much higher than LRIC prices when taking into consideration the value of the real options. However, these theoretically very valid critiques have not had much success with actual regulators, who either ignored them or, in rare cases, such as the UK, rejected them for legacy networks.

In contrast, for new networks, Hausman (1997) argues that access seekers receive a free option on the sunk investments of the incumbent, because they will only seek access if there is enough demand and pay nothing otherwise. He therefore suggests imposing a risk premium on the LRIC price to compensate for the value of this option. Bourreau et al. (2020b) have taken up this issue in a duopoly model with uncertainty by considering three potential remedies, the Hausman-type markup, the ex ante sale of an access option and the use of ex ante long-term contracts for wholesale access based on an LRIC price.[18] Systematically, the markup is a pure ex post remedy. The potential entrant only has to make an ex post decision, whether to enter or not. In contrast, the long-term contract is a pure ex ante remedy. The entrant makes an ex ante decision and is then committed to enter. The option remedy combines the two. The potential entrant has to make an ex ante decision to buy the option and an ex post decision to enter or not. In terms of competition, markups establish a high

---

[18] Inderst and Peitz (2014) also treat markups and long-term contacts. They do so in a model with variation in quality, while Bourreau et al. (2020b) model geographic coverage variations.

price under competition, prices under an exercised option will be lower because of the lack of markup, while prices under long-term contracts will be lowest because of the sunk nature of the entrant's access decision. Since the incumbent's coverage will be highest at the monopoly price, markups in general provide for the highest coverage followed by access options, while coverage under long-term contracts, because of the fierce ex post competition, is highly sensitive to the extent of uncertainty. The incumbent is rewarded ex ante but faces fierce competition ex post.

Dealing with New Technologies

The rigidity of cost-based pricing can become a problem when an old regulated technology competes with a new unregulated technology. In this case, the incumbent may have incentives to foreclose access seekers in spite of LRIC pricing of access: The actual costs of access are largely sunk and there is competitive pressure in the retail market. Thus, the incumbent would want to lower its end-user price below the costs measured by cost models, while the entrants have to buy wholesale access at LRIC based on such models. Since, from a normative perspective, the incumbent should be able to compete against the new technologies, it should be able to set competitive retail prices, but that would foreclose wholesale-dependent entrants. According to Briglauer and Vogelsang (2011), in such a case, the incumbent should be allowed to lower the retail price provided the wholesale access price is lowered as well in order to avoid a price squeeze. The access price would then be $a = min (LRIC, margin rule)$. A further advantage of this rule is that (at least in the short run) the regulator would not have to determine if the incumbent is still dominant in the new market environment.

An alternative approach by Neumann and Vogelsang (2013) can be applied if the incumbent also offers the new network service but is only regulated for the legacy service. In this case, the regulator can apply an opportunity cost approach in the spirit of Baumol (1983) to the relevant wholesale access price of the legacy service. This circumvents the issue that the forward-looking costs of the legacy service may vanish in light of sunkness and the prospect of no new investment in the legacy network. Specifically, Neumann & Vogelsang propose to price the old network access based on the modern equivalent asset (MEA) of the new network. Since the new network is technologically superior to the old one, the cost of the new network access (as a basis for pricing the old network access) should, however, be corrected by the performance delta between the two networks. Instead of using and measuring quality of service (QoS) differences, the authors determine the performance delta based on the market valuation of services provided over the old and the new network access represented by the end-user prices of services and corrected by cost differences downstream of the access provision. Under this approach, an access seeker becomes indifferent (on the margin) between using the old or the new access network and wholesale pricing (or regulation) becomes competitively neutral toward technology choice between the old and the new access.

Conclusions on Cost-Based Pricing

While rate-of-return regulation as a cost-based pricing approach was associated with potential over-investment, the new cost-based approaches to wholesale access pricing have raised the fear of too little investment and innovation. We have discussed some potential remedies in this section and will take up more in Section 5.3.

4.5.6 Yardstick Regulation and Benchmarking

An ideal regulatory system would, in the absence of externalities and public goods, mimic the outcome of competition. Monopoly regulation can only achieve that to a limited degree. However, in some cases, competition can replace part of the tasks of monopoly regulation. A particular case of pseudo competition is known as "yardstick regulation" or "benchmarking," which can be applied if there exist several monopoly firms in different geographic areas that are in the same jurisdiction of the regulator. If these firms are sufficiently similar to each other, the regulator can set the regulated price not only depending on the firm's own cost but also depending on the other monopolists' costs (Vogelsang, 1984; Shleifer, 1985).

The following example of the regulated price under the yardstick approach is due to Armstrong et al. (1994):

$$P_i(c_i, c_j) \leq \hat{P} + (1 - \rho)c_i + \rho \cdot \kappa \cdot c_j.$$

Here, $\hat{P} \geq 0$ is a markup to ensure viability of the firm; $0 \leq \rho \leq 1$ is a cost-sharing parameter. If $\rho = 0$, then the price for firm i only depends on its own cost, thereby mimicking rate-of-return regulation. If $\rho = 1$, then the price only depends on the cost of the other firm j, mimicking pure price caps.

The κ is the cost correlation between i and j. Thus, for given $0 < \rho < 1$, a high correlation between the cost of i and j gives the cost of j a higher weight for firm i's price. This correlation is applied because of the Armstrong et al. assumption that firm i only learns its type θ after choosing its cost-reducing effort e. Marginal cost is assumed to be $c = \theta - e$, where $\theta \in [\underline{\theta}, \overline{\theta}]$.

Benchmarking is a popular regulatory pricing approach closely related in spirit to yardstick regulation. Various methods are used, mostly for electricity distribution networks, where many monopoly firms can exist in a given country.

Total factor productivity analysis compares the total factor productivity of the various regulated monopolies and bases prices or the X-factor of price caps on the total factor productivity of the most productive firm or firms. This approach is very data intensive. Furthermore, the capital input is hard to measure and is often approximated by the dollar amounts spent on capital inputs.

Stochastic frontier analysis generates a regressed productivity or cost frontier based on a number of observations. In this case, a frontier is estimated based on a postulated functional form. This allows some observations to lie beyond the frontier and can be interpreted as stochastic influences rather than efficiency influences. It is again data intensive, but it is also well grounded in theory and estimation. In contrast, data envelope analysis is fairly simple and deterministic, but very sensitive to the influence of outliers, because all observations have to lie inside the frontier.

The problem of benchmarking lies in the heterogeneity of costs and demands between the different regulated firms. Only part of this heterogeneity can usually be explained by statistical methods so that inefficiencies and unexplained other differences often have to be lumped together.

Using a stochastic frontier analysis, Senyonga and Bergland (2018) find that yardstick regulation enhanced technical change and productivity growth of Norwegian electric utilities in 2007–12 relative to price cap regulation in 2004–6.

4.5.7 Coinvestment

Wholesale access regulation is often complicated and sometimes impossible. For example, it may be impossible to grant physical wholesale access to some telecommunications infrastructures. At the same time, the cost of duplicating the infrastructure may be wasteful or prohibitive. In such cases coinvestment by several competitors may still be feasible and may avoid some of the regulatory complications. Coinvestment, for example, has been widespread in the Swedish telecommunications sector both in the fixed and the mobile networks. Compared to infrastructure-based competition between firms owning separate infrastructures, coinvestment will usually save resources, although it will often be more costly than monopoly provision. Compared to downstream competition under wholesale access regulation, downstream competition between independently acting coinvestors will be fiercer, because the jointly owned network is sunk and carries almost zero access costs up to the capacity limit. Thus, the coinvestors face much lower short-run marginal costs than wholesale access seekers, whose marginal costs include the wholesale access charge (which also is an opportunity cost for the vertically integrated incumbent). Such fierce competition may be socially desirable, as long as the resulting prices cover the investment costs. However, in case of a small number of coinvestors who want to avoid such fierce competition, collusion is quite likely, as shown in experimental settings by Krämer and Vogelsang (2016).

Since policies incentivizing coinvestment usually aim at increasing investment or coverage, the question is how coinvestment compares to wholesale access-based investment and to unregulated monopoly. Bourreau et al. (2018) have addressed this question in a coverage game under uncertainty. In their case, unregulated monopoly always leads to the highest coverage, due to the low cost and high price of the monopolist. Next comes coinvestment and then wholesale access-based competition.

The new European Electronic Communications Code (EECC) to ultrafast broadband investment has favored coinvestment by – under certain conditions – exempting the coinvestors from wholesale access regulation, but has at the same time burdened coinvestment by stipulating that additional coinvestors have to be able to join even after the investment has been undertaken. These additional coinvestors receive a valuable option that they are only going to exercise if market conditions look good at that point in time. There are, however, no specific provisions in the EECC on pricing that would make it attractive for networks to initiate such investments in the first place if they have to provide open access to other parties. In particular, for open access to coinvestment, the regulators would have to make a 20/20 hindsight decision on the risk faced by the original investors. In my view, it will be almost impossible to ex post reconstruct the original risk faced by the original investors. Rather, the decision about coinvestment pricing for later entrants will have to be made ex ante.

Bourreau et al. (2020a) therefore suggest an approach that makes use of the real options theory mentioned previously and combines it with LRIC (or other cost-based) pricing of the coinvestment share. The idea is that ex post access to coinvestment or to shared assets will be granted at LRIC prices provided the access seeker presents an option certificate for such access. These option certificates will be sold at the time of the investment, at which time the original investors receive the sales revenue. Besides the sale of ex ante options, Bourreau et al. (2020a) consider LRIC pricing and LRIC pricing with a markup (as suggested by Hausman, 1997) as methods how such ex post entry might be accomplished. They use the coinvestment outcome without later entry as a benchmark and compare (a) cost-based entry, (b) cost-based entry with a markup and (c) cost-based entry with an ex ante option payment.

Their model based on Bourreau et al. (2018) addresses the coverage investment decision of an incumbent in a geographic model with continuously changing network population density. They assume that there is no price regulation and that coinvestment increases competition. Ex ante uncertainty about demand is resolved after the investment decision has been made. In such a model the monopoly coverage is the highest, because the monopolist can serve the lowest density, highest cost areas at monopoly prices. Lower cost areas will be served with coinvestment at competitive prices. The model shows that, under pure cost-based pricing, coverage will be lowest. In general, the option approach will not achieve the same coinvestment coverage as coinvestment without the possibility of ex post entry. The reason is that the potential coinvestor's willingness to pay for the option is less than the incumbent's loss from ex post coinvestment, because the exercise of the option increases competition. A markup on the cost of ex post entry can, in such cases, be superior for coverage because it will occur less often than the exercise of the option, which will already occur at less favorable demand states. Thus, Bourreau et al. (2020a) validate Hausman's (1997) conjecture, although the required markup is hard to determine. In contrast, the option can be sold ex ante in a market.

Thus, overall coinvestment may help overcome natural monopoly problems and lead to less wholesale access regulation, provided care is taken to prevent collusion and to provide open access with remedies.

4.6 Vertical Separation

As discussed earlier, vertical separation can eliminate the conflict of interest of the wholesale provider but may also sacrifice vertical economies. The strength of vertical economies, however, changes over time so that vertical separation may be a good regulatory move, once vertical economies weaken. For example, for several decades, cell towers were predominantly owned by the large mobile telephone operators, but then specialized firms emerged that, in the USA, are already dominating that input provision over integrated self-supply. Such developments are also envisaged in other network settings. These developments have led the EU in the EECC to incentivize vertically separated wholesale input supply by exempting it under certain circumstances from some regulatory obligations even if the suppliers are dominant in the wholesale market. They will have to offer their wholesale access services on a fair, reasonable and nondiscriminatory basis. The idea behind this move is that the formerly vertically integrated firms will only buy from the separate specialists if they find the purchase from wholesale-only firms to be more profitable and reliable. Thus, dominating wholesale-only firms face potential (re-) entry through backward integration of their wholesale buyers.

5 From Telecommunications to the Provision of ICT Services

5.1 Termination Monopoly

Special telecommunications topics arise from the reciprocal or two-way nature of telecommunications. Telephone calls or Skype calls go both ways. Two-way exchanges are not unheard of in other network industries. For example, electricity customers with solar panels may both take out of and feed into the public electricity grid. For telecommunications, such reciprocity, however, is the rule rather than the exception. As already explained, two-way communications lead to network externalities and call externalities. We now add the property of gatekeeper access and two-way access, which give rise to the termination monopoly and the net neutrality issue.

Different network operators often interconnect with and provide access to each other (called "termination" in telecom networks). This issue first arose at the international level between monopolistic national carriers. It gained a new and different quality under competition between networks serving the same geographic area. If they do not interconnect, as it happened in the early telephone history of the USA after the Bell patents expired, then subscribers may only be able to call other subscribers on the same network. The question is if interconnection between such networks should be mandated and regulated. The argument against a mandate and regulation is that networks have a natural incentive to interconnect in order to reap network effects (Spulber & Yoo, 2009). The argument for a mandate and for regulation is that large networks already internalize most of the possible network effects and can prevent competition by refusing to interconnect.[19]

In particular, interconnection as the basis for network competition is associated with call termination on other networks. This results in a termination monopoly if the receiving party can only be reached over one network. In this case, if the subscriber of a network originates a call to a party, the call can only be completed on the network of the called party, giving the originating network no choice. This termination monopoly is not dependant on the market power on the end-user side and is therefore called a "competitive bottleneck" (Armstrong, 2002).

There are three potential anticompetitive consequences of unregulated mutual termination between networks. The first is price collusion, because termination charges are marginal costs but largely cancel out as payments. Thus, a mutual increase in termination charges costs the firms little or nothing in terms of wholesale access payments but incentivizes them to charge higher

---

[19] This is related to the standardization issue in the economics of technical change treated by Katz and Shapiro (1985), who present the tradeoff between realizing network effects via compatibility and standardization on the one hand and product differentiation via incompatibility on the other.

end-user prices. Second, the termination charge can be a vehicle to increase market power by dominant firms. Third, under independent price setting by both firms, double marginalization may result.

The collusion result is based on three main assumptions. The first is reciprocity of the access price. This means that the two networks agree to charge each other the same price. The second is a balanced calling pattern. This means, if end-user prices on all networks are the same, the number (and length) of outgoing calls equals that of incoming calls for each individual network subscriber. The third assumption is that of linear and nondiscriminatory pricing downstream. Although the collusion result is quite intuitive and seems to have been empirically validated by the high termination charges in the mobile telephone industry before termination regulation, the result only holds under specific conditions. In particular, it only holds under linear pricing downstream, because under nonlinear pricing the networks can influence the subscription decisions and the usage decisions of end users with different pricing instruments and are thereby incentivized to attract subscribers by offering them a high surplus from usage.[20]

Under these three assumptions, if one firm charges a high access price, it will get a high margin on selling access service, but also will pay higher access costs to the other network. Due to same mutual charge and balanced calling patterns, each firm actually earns zero profit from selling the access service. As a result, without collusion, the firms will agree on reciprocal termination charges at a level that will lead to monopoly prices downstream. End users on both sides pay the monopoly price. (Armstrong, 1998; Laffont et al., 1998a)

Based on symmetric networks, instead of charging the same high price for each other, why not make it simple by charging no price at all? This approach is known as the "bill & keep" (B&K) system. It has early on been used between Internet backbone providers in the form of (unpaid) peering and has been suggested by policymakers for telephone call terminations. Most opposition against B&K has come from mobile operators and from fixed network incumbents. The argument by fixed network incumbents largely rests on the so-called hot potato problem illustrated in Figure 3.

Since firm 2 will have to pay the access price either way it routs the call, it will choose the minimum distance (solid line) within its network to save transportation cost, and let the other network deal with the rest. By handing over to the adjacent network 1 as quickly as possible, the firm can save network investment. While large incumbents have therefore mostly resisted B&K, there now is a natural move

---

[20] For differentiated assessments and comprehensive reviews of the collusion result, see Decker (2015) and Comino and Manenti (2014).

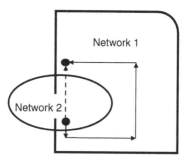

Figure 3 Hot potato problem

toward it caused by the prevalence of "over-the-top" services (OTTs). Digital convergence has led to the distinction between transport networks and the services delivered over them. OTTs compete successfully with ISPs in these services and have thereby destroyed the synergy advantages previously enjoyed by the network providers. To the extent that OTTs are themselves not subject to ISP termination charges, those charges become less and less viable, because OTTs can out-compete the legacy services that have to pay for termination and that apply usage-based charges to end users. Thus, substitute OTTs are likely to destroy this type of ISP gatekeeping, making B&K the probable future of legacy terminations (Vogelsang, 2017a). To the extent that OTTs cause a move toward B&K, the ISPs lose part of their service revenues and will therefore have to increase their subscriber charges, something that should be feasible, since the presence of OTTs increases the value of the ISP networks to the subscribers.[21]

While the USA has already moved toward a B&K system, the EU holds on to regulated termination charges and the possibility to regulate OTTs in order to establish a level playing field for ISPs. In my view, OTTs have enabled service competition for end users without requiring traditional interconnections. Thus, termination regulation, other than requiring B&K, would appear to be superfluous. Overcoming interest-group pressure and their own self-interest to continue regulation is difficult for regulators. It can therefore be helpful if OTTs do part of this work for them.

Similar conflicts between OTTs and other ICT-based services with regulation occur for end-user services in telephony, TV, taxis, house rentals etc. In all these cases, the ICT-based services offer imperfect and sometimes superior substitutes

---

[21] Specific discriminatory subscriber charges for OTTs themselves may be prevented by net neutrality rules described in the following. Overall end-user subscription charges, however, could be raised as demand for such subscription becomes more valuable. This possibility may be limited by competition, which is often influenced by the regulation of wholesale access charges. Thus, regulators may have to revisit such charges in response to OTT competition for ISP services.

to the legacy services they compete with. However, the legacy services are usually subject to stricter regulation than the ICT-based services. This conflict has led to calls for level playing fields in the form of similar regulation of the ICT-based services and/or (partial) deregulation of the legacy services. Since the new services increase competition in those markets, a move toward deregulation of market-power-based regulations, such as price regulations for taxis, appears to be in order. In contrast, externality-based regulations may be advisable on a case-by-case basis with harmonization that eliminates competitive distortions. Whether, for example, interconnection obligations should be imposed on services such as WhatsApp is questionable, because end users easily can multi-home and therefore be connected via other channels to the persons they wish to reach.

5.2 Net Neutrality

While for a long time the Internet has been remarkably free of regulation, it is fascinating to see that net neutrality (NN) regulation has emerged as a hot policy issue for the last fifteen years. The so-called netheads, who traditionally represent the regulation-free Internet, were the ones calling for NN regulation, while "bellheads," representing the traditionally regulated network companies, were fighting against NN regulation. NN is a postulate for ISPs to deliver content indiscriminately and without priority or special charges for content providers.

The NN issue resembles the termination monopoly issue, but is nonreciprocal. The *content service providers* (CSPs) need access to end users via ISPs that own the access networks. The ISPs act as platforms for end users and CSPs. This is a two-sided market issue and shows the key role of content for competition in the converged telecommunications sector.

The reasons why ISPs would violate NN principles are, in particular, (1) to manage capacity constraints (especially for mobile networks), (2) to extract content rents, (3) to reduce network competition (especially for fixed networks under convergence), and (4) to cater to network uses that require faster and/or more reliable service than the best-effort Internet. The first and fourth of these violations would tend to be welfare improving, while the second and third would tend to be welfare reducing.

As Vogelsang (2018b) remarks, the economics literature has been largely critical of NN regulation on the basis of theoretical findings that NN violations can be both welfare improving and welfare deteriorating, depending on the circumstances of the case in question. In particular, ISPs rarely have incentives to exclude content providers (Dewenter & Rösch, 2016). Thus, an ex post competition policy approach would be preferable to a strict ex ante prohibition of NN violations. In contrast, Vogelsang (2018b) argues that NN regulation is largely ineffective, in particular, when it comes to the prohibition of fast lanes and other quality of service (QoS) differentiations, and to a lesser extent, when it comes to the zero price rule. NN regulations are already being circumvented via other technologies available to large players who need, for example, higher QoS. A main reason for this bypass is that many content services require complementary network structures that will only be provided if they are profitable. To the extent that the ISP under NN rules cannot profitably provide those network structures, the content providers get them from other sources or provide their own.

In the future, for example via 5G, such bypass technologies are likely to be available to more players and will be associated with lower costs so that NN policies are likely to further lose their effects. NN regulation is effective only in preventing the blocking of specific content and in preventing the favoring of ISP-owned content and in preventing some price discriminations. These are also areas where NN regulations are more likely to be welfare enhancing. Where they are ineffective, NN regulations are likely to create extra costs and allocative inefficiencies caused by NN bypass.

5.3 Regulatory Paradigm Changes in Telecommunications and Beyond?

There are two major new developments that may require a regulatory paradigm change. The first is that the digital economy affects the management of all network industries, those that are directly associated with it and those that are not. The second and related development is that regulators put increasing emphasis on investment and innovation rather than on productive and allocative efficiency.

The digital economy has had or will have huge impacts on all network industries. Obviously this holds first of all for the telecommunications and communications networks that helped foster the digital economy. It next holds for electricity networks that are becoming "smart" and that now use almost real-time trading arrangements, something that was already foreseen by Vickrey (1971) and Schweppe et al. (1988). Real-time and more complex trading arrangements are gaining increasing importance because of the service nature of network services, the limited capacity of networks and the increasing capability of ICT (Newbery, 2018).

This increasing emphasis on ICT and the fact that remaining network bottlenecks tend to require large investments in new infrastructures, have led to an increasing emphasis of regulators on investment and innovation rather than on static allocative and productive efficiency.

The increasing emphasis on investment and innovation has major effects on the weights given, in particular, to the objective of enhancing competition and containing market power via wholesale access regulation. To the extent that the relevant investments/innovations are associated with near-natural monopoly characteristics infrastructure competition *in* the market is unlikely to work and policies advancing competition *in* the market may hinder competition *for* the market. Regulators have therefore introduced a number of new regulatory initiatives, represented by the EECC for telecommunications in Europe. These include the previously mentioned regulatory relief for some kinds of coinvestment and for wholesale-only businesses. Another new type of regulation concerns symmetric regulation for infrastructure sharing. Independent of market dominance, this kind of sharing obligation applies to infrastructures that are too costly to duplicate. Since this property very much resembles the natural monopoly requirement of essential facilities, the only difference from the essential facilities approach is that, in principle, competitors could survive without access to the facility. Thus, the main aim of this new regulation is to reduce the cost of new infrastructure development and thereby generate incentives for such investment. While voluntary asset sharing has for some time been commonplace in the mobile communications sector, the regulatory asset sharing in the fixed network sector is an obligation imposed on classes of assets independent of market dominance. It can therefore generate counter incentives if the conditions for symmetric access are unfavorable for the asset owners (Vogelsang, 2019). Symmetric regulation only makes sense in a network industry with a fairly large number of active players with different capabilities, such as the case of the telecommunications and ICT sector after a long time of market opening and after digital convergence and the emergence of OTTs. The new developments reflect and contribute to the complexity of the industry. They depend very much on private initiatives and change the role of the regulator from an active player to an arbitrator (Littlechild, 2009; Brousseau & Glachant, 2012).

For some transition period, regulators should not regulate dynamic new network features while continuing to regulate legacy networks. Vogelsang (2017b), for example, shows that abstaining from regulating a new network will enhance investment incentives for building such a network in a similar way as patents enhance innovation incentives. In both cases, end users may have to pay a high price but they will get the service. Continuing to regulate the old service may or may not boost investment incentives for the new service. In case of a simultaneous-move game, regulation of old services reduces the cannibalization effect for incumbent's innovation. By creating entrants with less cannibalization problems, such regulation facilitates the race for innovation between incumbent and entrants. It may even eliminate the cannibalization problem if the incumbent becomes a Stackelberg leader in the innovation game (Vogelsang, 2017b). This suggests that regulation of legacy networks and nonregulation of new innovative networks may be able to continue side by side.

5.4 Empirical Evidence on Telecommunications Policy Outcomes

Economists have criticized regulatory policies for a long time, but the empirical base for such criticisms has only more recently become rigorous. Early empirical work on telecommunications regulation, in particular, focused on pricing distortions caused by cross-subsidization of inelastic local telephone calls and subscriptions by much more elastic long-distance calls (Hausman, 1998, for the USA) and on regulatory delays of new services. For example, without regulatory delays, cellular mobile services in the USA could have started ten years earlier than they did and could have generated billions of dollars in benefits during that time (Hausman, 1997).

Empirically evaluating telecommunications policies can be extremely difficult, because (a) telecommunications services generate social benefits beyond the consumer surplus experienced by the immediate users or subscribers, (b) in view of fast technology changes, consistent time series are hard to come by, (c) telecommunications services are highly heterogeneous across countries, and (d) the role of preexisting infrastructures can be substantial. For all these reasons, many different yardsticks have been applied for measuring policy impacts. For example, as described previously, investment in new infrastructures is now a prime yardstick. Since investment is an input rather than an output, it can at best be a proxy for the value generated by new infrastructure. Data on investment are, however, more easily available than, for example, data on penetration and on prices (which have to apply to bundles of heterogeneous services). With that in mind, we here review some of the empirical findings, mostly for the EU and the USA, differentiating the mobile and the fixed line telecommunications sectors.

Mobile Communication

Mobile communication has come in generations that represent stages of technological developments. While the USA was among the pioneers for 1G, it fell behind the EU for 2G, which was associated with the enormous growth of mobile penetration. The European success of 2G was largely due to its focus on the Global System for Mobile Communications (GSM) as an EU-wide standard, while the USA left it to each of the mobile operators to choose a technology, because the major US-based carriers preferred different technologies (Cave et al., 2018). Because of its large installed 2G base and because of quitted 3G spectrum auctions the EU, however, lagged behind the USA in the penetration of 3G and

4G (Yoo, 2014). Looking forward, both the EU and the USA are trying hard to implement the new 5G standard with currently no victor in sight. Something to learn from this experience is that what appears to be success, in this case in terms of penetration, is path dependent and may change substantially over time.

Applying mobile usage as an alternative yardstick to penetration, Littlechild (2006) showed that the USA was way ahead of the EU during the 2G era. He ascribed this to the fact that the USA has a receiving-party-pays system for call termination and, as a result, largely vanishing mobile termination charges at the wholesale level. In contrast, the EU has a calling-party-pays system with initially very high wholesale termination charges that were reduced by regulation starting only in the late 1990s. This reduction in termination charges was associated with a waterbed effect, resulting in higher subscription charges and less promotion for subscriptions (Genakos & Valletti, 2011). This may have influenced lower penetration in the EU for some time. In contrast, at higher mobile penetration rates the waterbed effect no longer shows up, because more and more terminations occur between mobile networks rather than from mobile to fixed networks (Genakos & Valletti, 2015).

Fixed Networks

The policy successes in the fixed network sector have gone through similar waves in the USA and EU as in the mobile sector. For a long time, the USA was the clear policy leader, liberalizing long-distance telephony and telephone equipment already in the 1970s, long before the Europeans. This American lead lasted into the late 1990s, when unfortunate policy choices on regulatory unbundling obligations destroyed the US model of incentivizing service competition. In contrast, as described further in Section 6.2, in 2003, the EU came up with a systematic approach to regulation and deregulation that has been its policy for a long time. While being quite successful in guiding regulation and leading to an impressive amount of deregulation, it fell short of deregulating the main local networks of incumbent telephone companies. This turned out to be a handicap when it came to the provision of next-generation access networks (NGA). Here the USA took a lead by experimenting with a deregulated approach to infrastructure investment in fiber networks around 2003/2005.

Yoo (2014) observes a large difference between NGA availability in the USA and the EU in 2013, with an 82 percent coverage in the USA versus 54 percent coverage in the EU He suggests that this difference is due to the comparative absence of access regulation in the USA since around 2005. However, NGA coverage in the USA by cable TV companies accounts for 81 percent of the 82 percent, reflecting the vast geographic overlap between NGA coverage by cable TV and telephone companies. In contrast, cable TV coverage in the EU was only 39 percent. Thus, it is hard to disentangle the effect of cable TV (which faces no access regulation in either region) from nonregulation.[22] In my view, the economics of cable TV with its huge installed base was simply more favorable than converting the incumbents' copper access networks to NGA.

The Impact of Regulation on Investment in New Infrastructures

As a consequence of the policy emphasis for fixed networks on investment in new infrastructures, the empirical literature has also focused on the relationship between investment/innovation and regulation. Most of this work is empirically rigorous and emphasizes causality.

The first influential work on this issue, Grajek and Röller (2012), considers the effects of access regulation on new investments by incumbents and entrants. Their empirical estimations show a negative effect on incumbent investment and on investment overall, but only when regulation is taken to be endogenous. Their suspicion therefore is that regulators increase regulation in response to investment/innovation.

A more specific relationship concerns the effects of regulation of legacy networks on investment/innovation in NGA networks. The standard theoretical model on this issue by Bourreau et al. (2012) identifies three main effects which access price regulation of legacy networks will have on investment in new (next generation) networks. The *wholesale revenue effect* (or cannibalization or Arrow effect) induces more investment in new networks, because under regulation the old network becomes less attractive. In contrast, the *migration effect* makes the new network less attractive, because customers want to stay with the old network under the low regulated price. Furthermore, the *replacement effect* induces wholesale access seekers to invest in the new network only if the access charge is high. The overall effect of legacy regulation on innovation of new infrastructure therefore depends on parameter values, because the Arrow (= cannibalization) effect on the one hand and the replacement and migration effects on the other, coexist and work in opposite directions.

Briglauer (2015) and Briglauer and Cambini (2019) have shown empirically that, on average, the migration and replacement effects dominate so that less or softer legacy regulation would increase NGA investment. The analysis by Briglauer and Cambini (2019) applies to a sample of twenty-five EU member states using year 2003 to 2015 panel data on the adoption of fiber-based broadband technology by households and firms. Their results show that an increase in the regulated price for

---

[22] Legacy access regulation does not affect cable operators' investments in the EU (Briglauer et al., 2018).

accessing the old network favors consumer adoption of the new technology. In particular, they find that an increase in the unbundling price of 10 percent increases fiber-based adoption in the range of 0.7–1 percent. This effect of regulation of old networks on investment in new networks suggests that incumbents expect to be regulated, once they have done the NGA build-out. There is some contrary evidence by Bourreau et al. (2018), who show that regulated local loop unbundling incentivized fiber investment in a large sample of French municipalities.

Furthermore, according to Briglauer (2015) and Briglauer and Cambini (2019) the large installed base of high-quality copper access networks has been a handicap when it came to building new fiber-to-the-home (FTTH) access networks. The negative effects of the existing DSL base on NGA investments suggests cannibalization/sunk costs. Both the installed base effect and regulation are at fault for slowing down innovation. This explains why, for NGA networks, some low-income countries in Eastern Europe with a small asset base in legacy networks are currently ahead of high-income countries, such as Germany. These countries face less of a cannibalization problem, and legacy access regulation only applies to a small base.

Welfare Effects of New Infrastructures

A major question when measuring telecommunications policies by investment in new infrastructure or by penetration of new technologies is if the investment is worth its cost. Clearly, if consumers are willing to pay for these infrastructures by subscription and usage, it must be worth it to them. Nevertheless, the additional cost may not necessarily be worth replacing the previous infrastructure. Whether it is and, in particular, whether it justifies subsidies or cross-subsidies and the extra policy efforts, depends largely on additional benefits that the new technology provides. Quite a large amount of empirical work was conducted on benefits of regular broadband penetration starting with Röller and Waverman (2001) and culminating in Czernick et al. (2011), who investigate the effects of broadband adoption on GDP growth in twenty-five OECD countries during 1996 to 2007.[23] They suggest that the incremental value of broadband over narrowband services leads to a 2.7–3.9 percent GDP increase and that a 10 percent increase in broadband adoption in a country increases GDP growth by 0.9–1.5 percent. Using a microeconomic approach, Ahlfeldt et al. (2017) find that connecting unserved households and increasing speed would pass a cost-benefit test in urban and some suburban areas of the UK, though not necessarily in less densely populated areas. In a survey, Bertschek et al. (2016) provide more empirical evidence on specific benefits of broadband. This does

---

[23] For literature surveys on the evidence, see Cambini and Jiang (2009) and Briglauer et al. (2015).

not, however, mean that NGA (i.e., ultrafast broadband) also has an incremental value over regular broadband that justifies its incremental cost. First empirical work on this question for the EU for the 2003–15 period suggests a rather small but significant incremental value that would justify only about 50 percent coverage (Briglauer & Gugler, 2019). As Abardi and Cambini (2019) point out, larger network effects do not show up in this early work, because penetration of ultra-fast networks is still too small in the EU.

In their survey of empirical work, Bertschek et al. (2016) show that the effects of broadband services on employment and productivity strongly vary by economic sector and by skill levels. In general, broadband enhances employment and productivity in service industries and for higher skill levels but can have negative effects on the industrial sector and on low skill workers. This suggests that education and investment in skill levels might have to accompany policies incentivizing NGA infrastructure investments.

Overall, the empirical literature suggests (a) that new NGA infrastructure is desirable, (b) that subsidies for sparsely populated areas may be justified and (c) that it may be advisable not to regulate new infrastructure in areas not requiring subsidies.

5.5 Political Economy and Behavioral Aspects of Telecommunications Regulation

Our analysis so far assumes rational regulators pursuing welfare objectives. The empirical results discussed previously appear to be compatible with an approach wherein the negative outcomes of regulation for investment would be due to dynamic inconsistency of rational regulators. Deviations from such welfare-maximizing behavior could come from political economy or fairness considerations or from bounded rationality. Thus, Briglauer et al. (2019) find evidence supporting both regulators pursuing normative objectives and inefficiencies related to regulatory path dependence, bureaucracy goals and an inadequate consideration of competition from mobile broadband networks. Briglauer et al. (2019) do not specifically consider behavioral economic issues but those could also be responsible for their results. Both behavioral and political economy explanations of regulatory actions suggest that policy design needs a new impetus.

Until now, behavioral economics has found applications in regulations mostly for influencing firm and consumer behavior. Thus, regulators would use the insights of behavioral economics as their tool. In contrast, making the regulators themselves the subject of behavioral economics has been decidedly rare. Cooper and Kovacic (2012) combine political economy and behavioral economics, emphasizing regulatory and expert biases. Trillas (2016, 2020) focuses on the behavioral limitations to the regulators' rationality, pointing out that it can actually be beneficial to policy outcomes, for example, by overcoming free rider problems in the provision of public goods. Also, rational regulators have a hard time committing to not interfering after a firm has undertaken a sunk investment. In contrast, a regulator guided by fairness could do so.

Because of the required expertise for solving complex regulatory decision problems, Trillas (2020) suggests that regulatory agencies should have some independence from the political bodies. Because of potential expert bias, the independence should not be total, though. Trillas (2020) therefore suggests that expert bias should be countered by the use of a wider range of instruments. He notes that independent agencies are more stable when they enjoy public support and a high reputation, which appears to be paradoxical for an institution that is meant to be independent. Cambini and Rondi (2017) find for several European regulated industries that regulatory independence improves investment but does not eliminate effects of political interference. Hauge et al. (2012) argue that politicians use reappointment of regulators to discipline them in practice.

The policy consequences of behavioral economics for the choice of regulators and for regulatory procedures and institutional design are still quite general and need to become more specific in order to generate concrete prescriptions. Good general suggestions are to

(a) include behavioral biases in incentive schemes for regulators (Trillas, 2016),

(b) use negotiations with stake holders to reach regulatory decisions (Littlechild, 2009),

(c) make the independence of regulators accountable, as done in many countries by making them subject to potential court review,

(d) make regulatory decisions subject to an adversarial review (Cooper & Covacic, 2012), or

(e) reward outcomes of regulatory decisions rather than the decisions themselves.

Some practical approaches compatible with the behavioral model include the prescription of formalized input methodologies for regulatory costing and pricing in New Zealand. Such methodologies are the result of an elaborate process involving experts and stakeholders. They are binding and decisions based on them can be challenged in court. Lastly, they can only be changed with great effort.

Another behavioral issue concerns the decision between using replacement cost and historic cost for regulatory asset valuation. As Rogerson (2011) has shown, when applying the correct economic depreciation rate, both valuations are equivalent. Nevertheless, using historic cost complies better with the behavioral insights, because regulators then have a harder time expropriating the asset owner.

A further practical insight is that regulators often do not act on their better insights in changing a status quo even if they are convinced that it would be correct to change it. Examples include the decision to abandon highly inefficient cross subsidies in telephony or to maintain high termination charges. In both cases, emerging competition did the work for them and resolved the issue. Thus, allowing competition can help regulators achieve their objectives.

6 Deregulation and Competition Policy

6.1 Endgames Leading to Deregulation

Several developments have been responsible for increases in competition in network industries. In particular, new technologies and old (regulation-induced) inefficiencies have been driving forces for competition. [24] As an example of the latter, cross subsidies and inefficient operation have been a very common starting point. Furthermore, regulatory policies on wholesale services can jump-start competition. Interconnection and open access have been key. Liberalization and competition lead to at least an interim increase in regulation. Looking at such developments, one may wonder if a stable endgame is possible either in the form of stable regulation or of a deregulated state. In fact, there are now network industries with little or no market-power-based regulation, such as the airline industry in many countries. However, even there parts of the industry remain regulated, such as airports, which can be seen as nodes to a network. A casual observation of successful deregulation in network industries reveals that most of it occurred outside what Decker (2015) calls core networks. Examples besides the airlines include end-user services and terminal equipment in telephony and electricity generation and sales in some countries. In the telecommunications sector, long-distance networks have also been widely deregulated.

Industry-specific regulation of network industries potentially passes through four phases. In the first phase, market failures or distributional issues lead to the establishment of economic regulation. In this phase, there typically is an incumbent monopoly position, but in some cases, like that of airlines, competition may exist. This regulation phase may persist for a long time, often half a century. In the second, liberalization phase competition is allowed and, in

---

[24] This section partially draws on Vogelsang (2017a) and Vogelsang and Cave (2019).

former monopoly cases, it is most often associated with asymmetric regulation for wholesale bottleneck access. In the third phase, competition emerges in nonbottleneck areas, which are then deregulated. In the fourth phase, competition for bottlenecks appears and wholesale access is deregulated. Some network industries skip or compress some of the phases, and some industries never reach the fourth phase. Endgame regulation concerns either policies that lead to the fourth phase or policies in the third phase that lead to deregulation or keep the third phase stable.

In telecommunications, the original monopoly positions of the telephone incumbents were reached by a combination of economies of scale, sunk costs and network externalities. An infrastructure endgame leading to phase 4 may here be possible because of duplicate infrastructures made feasible by digital convergence and by fixed-mobile substitution and convergence. A service endgame (phase 3) may be possible because of the emergence of OTTs. However, as explained in Section 6.4, some of the OTTs may generate a new cycle for regulation to the extent that they benefit from strong network effects combined with economies of scale and sunk costs. For example, besides benefiting from strong network effects, the striking feature of Google's search engine strategy seems to be to create endogenous sunk costs in the sense of Sutton (1991) by continuously investing in new search features that make it hard for competitors to follow and, in particular, for newcomers to enter the market.

Deregulation has been an evergreen desire for many economists. The rationale for wanting to deregulate is the belief that competition is best for efficiency and innovation. However, wholesale regulation was meant to create and spur competition in legacy monopoly industries. So, why then deregulate? Deregulation is in order if the policy to spur competition, or technical and market changes, have created self-sustaining competition that can better be guarded by competition policy than by industry-specific regulation.

Deregulation decisions are linked in two crucial ways with the questions of whether, where, when and how to promote competition (Vogelsang & Cave, 2019). First, if competition is found to be sufficient and stable enough for deregulation, there is no further need to promote competition through regulatory tools. The market can be deregulated. Second, if the conditions for deregulation are not fulfilled, the promotion of competition may be in order. In that case, the ultimate goal may be to create sufficiently stable competition to permit deregulation. Although originally not designed for that purpose the so-called ladder of investment was interpreted by many, such as the European Commission, as a first systematic attempt for a dynamic policy that starts with liberalization cum asymmetric regulation and ends with deregulation of the incumbent. The basic idea is to successively provide entrants with higher levels of access that require more and more network investments by entrants, as the entrants climb higher rungs of the ladder. At the same time, the conditions for accessing the lower rungs are successively made more difficult so that entrants have incentives to leave the lower and climb the higher rungs. Whether entrants actually climb the ladder has been subject to some empirical testing. There is some empirical evidence that they do, at least partially (Bacache et al., 2014; Nardotto et al., 2015). Unfortunately, in many cases, the highest achievable rung still involves regulated access and therefore stops short of deregulation. Fortunately, coinvestment can be interpreted as a further rung to the ladder (ARCEP, 2019). While the "ladder of investment approach" has been controversial as a tool to generate full-fledged infrastructure competition, it has proven useful as a guide toward a dynamic escalation of remedies during the market development (Cave, 2014).

Does an endgame require deregulation? One can imagine a stable natural monopoly technology without the feasibility of infrastructure-based network competition. This could lead to a sustainable regulated and/or government-owned monopoly, such as in Australia and New Zealand. This would then be a regulated core, while the surrounding infrastructures and services could be deregulated.

6.2 Conditions for Deregulation

Today the scope for regulation and deregulation differs considerably between the various network industries; for example, between electricity and telecommunications. This shows up in differing approaches for the two industries. As a case in point, the EU telecommunications framework is based on steps toward deregulation, while the electricity framework is not. In judging the prospective chances of deregulation for a network industry, one has to establish under what conditions deregulation may be in order and whether those conditions are likely to apply now or in the future.

The evaluation standard for deregulation proposed here is that the state and expected development of competition are such that competition policy can deal with the problems arising in such markets in a better way than regulation can. In a market economy, industry-specific regulation is the exception, and markets only subject to competition policy are the rule. In the most relevant wholesale markets, competition policy can deal with most problems of noncompetitive market structures and behaviors. As explained in the following, it cannot deal with some particularly pervasive problems of network industries, such as persistent monopoly, however. For deregulation decisions, the counterfactual yardstick should be whether continued competition can be expected under deregulation.

The failure of the essential facilities doctrine in antitrust clearly shows that for essential facilities competition policy does not work (Areeda, 1989) and that therefore access regulation is warranted. The essential facilities approach to deregulation turns this argument around to call for deregulation if a facility no longer is deemed essential. This is a very sharp criterion that sets a high standard for regulation and a lenient standard for deregulation, since it would prescribe deregulation already if a facility is duplicated or if there exists another type of facility that allows for duopoly competition downstream.

The European framework for regulation of electronic communication services (ECS) came into force in 2003. This regime was perceived as a major step down the transition path between regulated monopoly and normal competition, governed exclusively by generic competition law. The regulations that may be imposed under the regime mostly require a demonstration that an operator has significant market power (SMP). Its provisions are applied across a range of "electronic communications services." It thus represented from the outset an attempt to corral the NRAs down the path of deregulation – but allowing them, however, to proceed at their own pace (but within the uniform framework necessary for the EU internal market).

Under so-called Directives, the European Commission first establishes and then from time to time revisits a list of markets where ex ante regulation is permissible, the markets being defined according to normal competition law principles.[25] These market definitions are then adapted and analyzed by NRAs with the aim of identifying SMP (on a forward-looking basis). The SMP can be exercised by a single firm, by two or more firms jointly ("collective dominance") or it can be transmitted from one market into a vertically related one. Where no dominance is found, ex ante obligations may not be imposed on any undertaking in the relevant market, but ex post competition law would still apply. Where dominance is found, the choice of an appropriate regulatory remedy must be made from a specified list.

Thus the effect of the regime is to create a series of market-by-market "sunset clauses" which reduce the level of ex ante regulation as the scope of effective competition expands.

In particular, the Recommendation operates by applying three cumulative criteria for identifying those markets that are deemed suitable for ex ante regulation:

---

[25] The European experience shows that it may be hard or impossible to use a cleanly defined market concept for this purpose (Hellwig, 2008). However, the search for such market and the policy-based determination of it have proven to be valuable.

1. High and nontransitory barriers to entry over the period of application of remedies,
2. The expected persistence of such barriers to entry beyond that period (making the prospect of effective competition unlikely), and
3. The inability of competition law adequately to address the particular issue;

The second of these is simply a projection into the more distant future of the first (albeit difficult to apply in practice). The third, cumulative, criterion is whether competition law is sufficient to address the particular market failures of criteria 1 and 2. To the best of our knowledge, criterion 3 has never been seriously analyzed in terms of the tradeoffs between using competition policy and ex ante industry-specific regulation. This is of obvious importance because, in a particular country, regulation policy can be strong and competition policy weak or, vice versa, competition policy can be strong and regulation can be weak.

Pursuant to Article 16 of the Framework Directive,[26] the regulatory framework only permitted the imposition of ex ante regulation where one or more undertakings are found to have significant market power in a market fulfilling all three of the criteria. The definition of SMP is identical to the standard definition of dominance determined and repeated by the European Court of Justice, but with the major difference that it is applied on a forward-looking basis. Since cumulative presence of the three conditions mentioned, plus a firm with SMP, are the conditions for regulation, the EU framework recommends deregulation if at least one of the criteria is not fulfilled (or if there is no firm with SMP).

The EU deregulation framework is conceptually elegant and clear. However, to our view, criterion 3 of the three-criteria test is excessively vague and needs to be replaced by a more involved test that compares regulation and competition policy, resulting in an "augmented" criterion 3. In particular, criterion 3, in its current form, never spelled out why competition policy cannot deal with the problems caused by criteria 1 and 2, while regulation can. It also deals with this as a "can" or "cannot" question, while both policies are sufficiently imperfect so that their abilities only differ by degree.

We here take a generic approach toward deregulation of wholesale markets as the starting point.[27] The measuring rod for deregulation is the answer to the question, can competition policy better achieve the policy goals than

---

[26] DIRECTIVE 2002/21/EC OF THE EUROPEAN PARLIAMENT AND OF THE COUNCIL of 7 March 2002 on a common regulatory framework for electronic communications networks and services (Framework Directive), https://eur-lex.europa.eu/legal-content/EN/TXT/PDF/?uri=CELEX:32002L0021&from=en.

[27] The following draws on Vogelsang (2017a).

regulation? Given that competition policy is supposed to maintain and spur competition, how does it differ from regulation? Table 1 contrasts features of regulation with those of competition policy, where in column 1 the properties of regulation are emphasized, while competition policy is viewed as possessing the opposite properties, meaning that competition policy imposes ex post remedies, is handled by a generalist agency and is unable to impose prescriptive interventions on pricing and quality. In contrast to regulation, competition policy – being very general – implies great adaptability to new industries and situations, but it has a limited set of industry-specific policy tools.

Table 1 brings out the tension between the potential of industry-specific regulation to be effective in having strong influence and in preventing harm, and its restriction of the freedom of regulated firms to compete and to appropriate the benefits of innovations.

Do the drawbacks of regulation alluded to in Table 1 mean that competition policy is better than regulation? The answer both varies by individual market and depends on the corresponding properties of competition policy. For present purposes, we confine the discussion to wholesale markets. Table 2 therefore points out the limitations for a move toward general competition law. In particular, if, under deregulation, systemic abuses by dominant firms with large, irreparable damages can be expected and if they cannot be deterred by competition policy penalties then regulation remains preferable. This holds, in particular, for genuine essential facilities or bottlenecks, which competition policy cannot deal with adequately (Areeda, 1989). Competition policy also cannot address external effects that do not affect competition. Furthermore, while regulation tends to delay activities by regulated firms that require regulation, competition policy will rarely be faster than regulation, although the effects of competition policy delays will be different. They will delay remedies, meaning that competition policy can be subject to substantial uncertainties, but will, in most cases, be less constraining on the behavior of dominant firms.

In the case of infrequent and ambiguous abuses, competition policy would normally resort to a rule-of-reason approach. In that case, ex ante regulation is unlikely to be better, because the behavior to be sanctioned can be good or bad, depending on the circumstances. In contrast, in cases of frequent abuses with clearly inefficient consequences, competition policy suggests a per se rule. In such cases, ex ante regulation may or may not be better than competition policy. It may be better because it prevents abuses directly and can be applied on a continuous basis. However, competition policy in such cases may be very predictable and could therefore effectively use penalties to deter bad behavior.

Table 1 Properties of regulation and competition policy

Properties of regulation in contrast to competition policy	Advantages	Drawbacks
• Ex ante remedies	• Potential immediacy • Dependability, precision, prevention of harm	• Often drawn-out decisions, slow to let go of status quo • Reduction of freedom to compete and innovate • Unjustified interventions
• Specialized industry-specific agency	• Specialized knowledge, speed of intervention	• Influence of interest groups; concern with distributional issues • Too specialized, expert bias • Too much (or too little) regulation
• Prescriptive intervention (affirmative duties) • Pricing • Quality setting	• Strong influence on desired behavior, precision • Dependability • Can treat externalities	• Reduction of freedom to compete and innovate • Inefficiencies from asymmetric information • Too much intervention

Table 2 Inappropriateness of general competition law

Property of competition law	Competition law inappropriate if	Competition law is inappropriate for . . .
• Requirement to prove violation can take long time, lowering deterrence	• Large, irreparable damages *(compensated by large penalties = deterrence?)* • Difficult and lengthy to prove abuses in changing environment • Frequent and repeated abuses	• Access to monopolistic bottlenecks • Predation against and foreclosure of competitors • Abuses in fast-changing markets

Table 2 (cont.)

Property of competition law	Competition law inappropriate if	Competition law is inappropriate for . . .
• Inability to set prices	• Lack of comparable markets • Economies of scale and scope • Long duration of intervention in a changing environment	• Access to monopolistic bottlenecks • Market dominance in access market • Monopoly in end-user market
• Inability of supervision	• High information requirements • Continuous supervision requirements	• Access obligations • Price regulation
• Inability to deal with externalities	• Externalities unrelated to competition/market power	• Interconnection • Environmental issues

Tables 1 and 2 suggest that the application of criterion 3 of the EU framework depends on the strength of the regulatory agency and the competition policy of the particular country.

A major discussion has evolved in the European telecommunications regulation about the question if tight oligopolies should be subject to regulation or not. According to the EU rules, joint SMP would signify that regulation might be warranted. In contrast, tight oligopolies are viewed as cases with independent behavior but strong recognition of mutual interdependence. The USA, since about 2005, has clearly taken the view that because of the investment objective, two separate infrastructure firms are enough for deregulation. Briglauer and Vogelsang (2017) have taken the view that for the EU, two infrastructure-based competitors should be enough if there are competitive safeguard functions and sufficiently strong competition law. They suggest that three independent network operators should definitely qualify for deregulation. The weakness of using tight oligopolies as a criterion for regulation is (a) that it neglects the upside potential for investments relative to the downside potential of static inefficiencies and (b) that noncompetitive behavior under tight oligopolies is not certain and can be handled by competition policy.

Thus, deregulation is in order if competition has developed to such an extent that predicted market failures can be dealt with by competition policy agencies and other general policies.

6.3 Digital and Fixed-Mobile Convergence as Causes for Deregulation

Sometimes the configuration of networks changes. In principle, networks could be split up into new networks or could merge into a combined type of network. Such developments raise interesting policy issues. Digital convergence belongs to the latter type of combining different types of networks in such a way that the resulting networks now belong to the same type. In this case, as a result of technical change, telephone networks, TV networks and data networks converged into one type of digital network that now can, in principle, supply all the services of the previously specialized networks.[28] This convergence meant that, even if the legacy networks represented monopolies, competition after network digitization became feasible for all these services. It further raised policy questions, since the legacy networks were governed by different institutional setups and regulatory rules. In particular, such policy issues arose for cable TV and telephone companies. Regulation of cable TV comes from the media side, which is mostly concerned with social and cultural issues, while telephone regulation is mostly concerned with containment of market power and reaching universal access. There are essentially three options for such a situation. The first is to continue regulating each legacy network as before. The second is to find a common regulatory setup for all of them. The third is to deregulate.

The USA has more or less pursued all these approaches.[29] First, cable networks, telephone networks and data networks continued to be regulated under their own rules. This, however, led to tension in the age of broadband, when wholesale access services were regulated for telephone networks, but not for cable TV networks, and wholesale data networks were regulated under their own rules. The USA is characterized by facilities-based broadband duopolies throughout most of the country with cable TV having the larger market share. Because the dominant cable networks are not regulated and in order to incentivize fiber investment, the USA has, since 2005, had no effective unbundling requirements for fixed telecommunications networks. However, starting around 2008 and formalized in 2015, telephone

---

[28] The digital convergence following from the move from analog to digital networks was made possible by standardization for packet switching.

[29] For a more extensive discussion of these US developments and the contrast to the EU, see Vogelsang (2015).

and cable TV networks were both regulated as common carriers for Internet services under NN rules. Last, since 2017, NN rules were given up altogether.

A complementary development to digital convergence is fixed-mobile convergence along with fixed to mobile substitution. Together they mean that several network infrastructures are now available in many areas so that deregulation could be in order. With the exception of the USA, this has hardly happened. The reasons to this are twofold. First, while being close substitutes, the various networks are still only imperfect substitutes both in demand and supply. They have different cost characteristics and different quality attributes, such as mobility, reliability, start-up speed etc. Regulators have therefore not become convinced that the different networks supply the same markets. Second, outside densely populated areas, only one or two networks are available so that deregulation in rural areas still may not work.

6.4 New Regulation for New Economy Networks?

While deregulation for physical telecommunications and communications networks has been on the policy agenda for quite some time, new regulation of ICT companies has become a new agenda. It relates to characteristics and behavior of the large Internet companies, the big four GAFA (Google, Amazon, Facebook, and Apple) in particular. These companies are highly profitable and they exert enormous economic and political influence. This influence includes market power in the traditional sense but also power that is not captured by market share or pricing behavior. In the case of Facebook, the power is associated with network externalities that are the essence of social networks. Network externalities or network effects are also important for the other three firms. In addition, all of them command a treasure trove of data that they can use. The network effects are a major reason for potential market tipping, because a network with already many subscribers can out-compete a network with fewer subscribers even if the latter provides superior services.

Until now, the market power problems caused by these firms have been dealt with through competition policy. For example, the EU has aggressively fought anticompetitive behavior of these firms, Google in particular. EU countries now consider creating new competition policy tools with a distinct regulatory taste and also consider outright regulation of these firms. The EU had previously taken strong regulatory steps on data privacy that was not so much restricted to these firms but was thought to apply to them. On the academic side, Lehr and Sicker (2018) and Lehr et al. (2019) have suggested a new regulatory approach, creating a new regulatory agency they have named *new*FCC, which should be in charge of more conventional asset sharing and access regulation and also of the Internet ecosystem focusing on multilayered platforms, such as the GAFA. They use the strong argument that market power issues transcend the various layers, the prime example being the competition between OTTs and ISPs for services. They suggest that the *new*FCC should use information and discourse as well as soft interventions, such as nondiscrimination rules, rather than conventional common carrier regulation for digital network platforms. The primary justification for creating the *new*FCC would be its expertise in creating focal points for decision-making.

7 Conclusions

This Element covers policy developments of network industries starting from utility-type monopoly regulation, moving on to liberalization and bottleneck regulation and ending with deregulation accompanied by competition policy. In the course of these developments, which network industries have gone through or are going through, the various industries have become more complex with many different players interacting horizontally and vertically.

Because of these developments, it is worth taking a new look at the regulation of network industries. In particular, network effects favor an increasing emphasis on investment and innovation as the major goals of regulation rather than static allocative and productive efficiency. Furthermore, the increasing dynamism in network markets requires flexible adaptation of policies. This is something neither competition policy nor industry-specific regulation can deal with very well. On top of that, ICT has an increasing influence on business models of networks and services that conflicts with conventional regulation. Besides those networks that are already part of ICT, such as telecommunications and cable TV networks, this most strongly concerns electricity distribution ("smart grids"), but also holds for roads (e.g., for autonomous vehicles) and other transportation networks.

Keys to the success of competition and deregulation are reductions in economies of scale and scope relative to market size. This could come from new technologies with less economy of scale and from growth of market size. A lack of strong vertical economies allows for separation of potentially competitive production stages. This usually requires successful wholesale regulation by the development of sufficiently simple and manageable wholesale products. Externalities can be dealt with separately for interconnection requirements and environmental regulation.

As vertical economies have weakened, network industries have become more complicated, because vertical relationships have been replaced by (at least initially regulated) markets. The complexity of regulation increases in the variety of types of competition and technologies. Furthermore, externality regulation may increase. Examples include termination charges and NN regulation. Accompanying this increase in complexity has been the developments of platforms as two-sided or multi-sided markets. This is most pronounced in the telecommunications and communications sectors but is catching on in other network industries, such as electricity (Weiller & Pollitt, 2013).

Traditional "public utility" industries have been slow moving and therefore been associated with stable regulation emphasizing static efficiency and fairness. In contrast, modern network industries are inherently dynamic, thereby requiring a regulatory paradigm change toward investment and innovation. Innovations and sunk investments are inherently risky and become riskier under regulatory uncertainty. Thus, they can be enhanced by regulatory commitment, something that is difficult in the fast-changing regulatory environments of our time. In principle, deregulation is a particularly strong commitment device from the regulatory perspective.

References

Abrardi, L., & Cambini, C. (2019). "Ultra-fast broadband investment and adoption: A survey." *Telecommunications Policy* 43(3): 183–198.

Ahlfeldt, G., Koutroumpis, P., & Valletti, T. (2017). "Speed 2.0: Evaluating access to universal digital highways." *Journal of the European Economic Association* 15: 586–625.

ARCEP (2019). "New code, new challenges for the Gigabit society: A French eye on the issues." Presentation by Emmanuel Gabla at the WIK Conference, October 15, www.wik.org/fileadmin/Konferenzbeitraege/2019/Gigabit_society/Gabla_2019–10-08_Presentation-WIK_v4.pdf.

Areeda, P. (1989). "Essential facilities: An epithet in need of limiting principles." *Antitrust Law Review* 58: 841–869.

Armstrong, M. (1998). "Network interconnection in telecommunications." *Economic Journal* 108: 545–564.

Armstrong, M. (2002). "The theory of access pricing and interconnection." In S. Majumdar, M. Cave, & I. Vogelsang (eds.), *Handbook of Telecommunications Economics*, Vol. 1, North-Holland Elsevier, 295–384.

Armstrong, M., & Sappington, D. E. M. (2007). "Recent developments in the theory of regulation." In M. Armstrong, & R. Porter (eds.). *Handbook of Industrial Organization*, Vol. 3, Elsevier B.V.

Armstrong, M., Cowan, S., & Vickers, J. (1994). *Regulatory reform: Economic analysis and British experience*. Cambridge, MA: MIT Press.

Armstrong, M., Doyle, C., & Vickers, J. (1996). "The access pricing problem: A synthesis." *Journal of Industrial Economics* 44: 131–150.

Averch, H., & Johnson, L. L. (1962). "Behavior of the firm under regulatory constraint." *American Economic Review* 52: 1052–1069.

Bacache, M., Bourreau, M., & Gaudin, G. (2014). "Dynamic entry and investment in new infrastructures: Empirical evidence from the fixed broadband industry." *Review of Industrial Organization* 44: 179–209.

Baron, D. P., & Myerson, R. B. (1982). "Regulating a monopolist with unknown costs." *Econometrica* 50: 911–930.

Baumol, W. J. (1983). "Some subtle issues in railroad regulation." *Journal of Transport Economics* 10: 1–2.

Baumol, W. J., Koehn, W. F., & Willig, R. D. (1987). "How arbitrary is arbitrary, or: Towards the desired demise of full cost allocation." *Public Utilities Fortnightly* 120(5): 16–21.

Belleflamme, P., & Peitz, M. (2015). *Industrial Organization: Market and Strategies*. 2nd ed., Cambridge, UK: Cambridge University Press.

Bernier, L., Florio, M., & Bance, P. (eds.) (2020). *The Routledge Handbook of State-Owned Enterprises*. London: Routledge.

Bertschek, I., Briglauer, W., Hüschelrath, K., Kauf, B., & Niebel, T. (2016). "The economic impacts of broadband internet: A survey." *Review of Network Economics* 14: 201–227.

Blackmon, B.G. (1992). "The incremental surplus subsidy and rate-of-return regulation." *Journal of Regulatory Economics* 4: 187–196.

Bose, A., Pal, D., & Sappington, D. E. M. (2017). "Pricing to preclude sabotage in regulated industries." *International Journal of Industrial Organization* 51: 162–184.

Bourreau, M., Cambini, C., & Doğan, P. (2012). "Access pricing, competition, and incentives to migrate from "old" to "new" technology." *International Journal of Industrial Organization* 30: 713–723.

Bourreau, M., Cambini, C., & Hoernig, S., (2018). "Cooperative investment, access, and uncertainty." *International Journal of Industrial Organization* 56: 78–106.

Bourreau, M., Cambini, C., Hoernig, S., & Vogelsang, I. (2020a). "Co-investment, uncertainty, and opportunism: Ex-ante and ex-post remedies." *CESifo Working Paper Series* 8078, CESifo Group Munich, January.

Bourreau, M., Cambini, C., Hoernig, S., & Vogelsang, I. (2020b). "Fibre investment and access under uncertainty: Long-term contracts, risk premia and access options." *Journal of Regulatory Economics* 57(2): 105–117.

Bourreau, M., Grzybowski, L., & Hasbi, M. (2018). "Unbundling the incumbent and entry into fiber: Evidence from France." *CESifo Working Paper Series* 7006, CESifo Group Munich.

Braess, D. (1969). "Über ein Paradox aus der Verkehrsplanung." *Unternehmensforschung* 12: 258–268.

Braeutigam, R. R. (1980). "An analysis of fully distributed cost pricing in regulated utilities." *Bell Journal of Economics* 11: 182–196.

Bresnahan, T. F., & Trajtenberg, M. (1995). "General purpose technologies 'Engines of Growth'?" *Journal of Econometrics* 65: 83–108.

Briglauer, W. (2015). "How EU sector-specific regulations and competition affect migration from old to new communications infrastructure: Recent evidence from EU27 member states." *Journal of Regulatory Economics* 48: 194–217.

Briglauer, W., & Cambini, C. (2019). "Does regulation of basic broadband networks affect the adoption of new fiber-based broadband services?" *Industrial and Corporate Change* 28: 219–240.

Briglauer, W., & Gugler, K. (2019). "Go for gigabit? First evidence on economic benefits of (ultra-) fast broadband technologies in Europe." *Journal of Common Market Studies* 57(5): 1071–1090.

Briglauer, W., & Vogelsang, I. (2011). "The need for a new approach to regulating fixed networks." *Telecommunications Policy* 35: 102–114.

Briglauer, W., & Vogelsang, I. (2017). "A regulatory roadmap to incentivize investment in new high-speed broadband networks." *DigiWorld Economic Journal* 106: 143–160.

Briglauer, W., Camarda, E. M., & Vogelsang, I. (2019). "Path dependencies versus efficiencies in regulation: Evidence from 'old' and 'new' broadband markets in the EU." *Telecommunications Policy* 43(8): 101825.

Briglauer, W, Cambini, C., and Grajek, M. (2018). "Speeding up the Internet: Regulation and investment in European fiber optic infrastructure." *International Journal of Industrial Organization* 61: 613–651.

Briglauer, W., Frübing, S., & Vogelsang, I. (2015). "The impact of alternative public policies on the deployment of new communications infrastructure: A survey." *Review of Network Economics*, 13: 227–270.

Brousseau, E., & Glachant, J.-M. (2012). "Regulating networks in the 'New Economy': Organizing competition to share information and knowledge." In E. Brousseau, M. Marzouki, & C. Meadel (eds). *Governance, Regulations and Powers on the Internet*. Cambridge: Cambridge University Press, 63–92.

Cambini, C., & Jiang, Y. (2009). "Broadband investment and regulation: A literature review." *Telecommunications Policy* 33: 559–574.

Cambini, C., & Rondi, L. (2017). "Independent agencies, political interference and firm investment: Evidence from the European Union." *Economic Inquiry* 55: 281–304.

Cave, M. (2014). "The ladder of investment in Europe, in retrospect and prospect." *Telecommunications Policy* 38: 674–683.

Cave, M., Genakos, C., & Valletti, T. (2018). 'The European framework for regulating telecommunications: A 25-year appraisal." *Review of Industrial Organization* 55: 47–62.

Coase, R. H. (1937). "The nature of the firm." *Economica* 4: 386–405

Comino, S., & Manenti, F. M. (2014). *Industrial Organization of High-Technology Markets*. Cheltenham, UK, and Northampton, MA: Edward Elgar.

Cooper, J. C., & Kovacic, W. E. (2012). "Behavioral economics: Implications for regulatory behavior." *Journal of Regulatory Economics* 41: 41–58.

Czernich, N., Falck, O., Kretschmer, T., & Woessmann, L. (2011). "Broadband infrastructure and economic growth." *Economic Journal* 121: 505–532.

Decker, C. (2015). *Modern Economic Regulation*. Cambridge, UK: Cambridge University Press.

Dewenter, R. & Rösch, J. (2016). "Net neutrality and the incentives (not) to exclude competitors." *Review of Economics* 67: 209–229.

Evans, L., & Garber, S. (1988). "Public utility regulators are only human: A positive theory of rational constraints." *American Economic Review* 78: 444–462.

Evans, L., & Guthrie, G. (2012). "Price-cap regulation and the scale and timing of investment." *Rand Journal of Economics* 41: 537–561.

Faulhaber, G.R. (1975). "Cross-subsidization: Pricing in public enterprises." *American Economic Review* 65: 966–977.

Florio, M. (2013). *Network Industries and Social Welfare*. Oxford: Oxford University Press.

Gasmi, F., Kennet, D. M., Laffont, J.-J., & Sharkey, W. W. (2002a). *Cost Proxy Models and Telecommunications Policy*. Cambridge, MA, and London: MIT Press.

Gasmi, F., Laffont, J.-J., & Sharkey, W. W. (2002b). "The natural monopoly test reconsidered: An engineering process-based approach to empirical analysis in telecommunications." *International Journal of Industrial Organization* 20: 435–459.

Genakos, C., & Valletti, T. (2011). "Testing the 'waterbed' effect in mobile telephony." *Journal of the European Economic Association* 9: 1114–1142

Genakos, C., & Valletti, T. (2015). "Evaluating a decade of mobile termination rate regulation." *The Economic Journal* 125, 586: F31-F48.

Geradin, D., & Sidak, G.F. (2005). "European and American approaches to antitrust remedies and the institutional design of regulation in telecommunications." In S. Majumdar, M. Cave & I. Vogelsang (eds.). *Handbook of Telecommunications Economics*, Vol.2. North-Holland Elsevier: 517–553.

Grajek, M., & Röller, L. H. (2012). "Regulation and investment in network industries: Evidence from European telecoms." *Journal of Law and Economics* 55: 189–216.

Hauge, J. A., Jamison, M. A., & Prieger, J. E. (2012). "Oust the louse: Does political pressure discipline regulators?" *Journal of Industrial Economics* 60: 299–232.

Hausman, J. (1997). "Valuing the effect of regulation on new services in telecommunications." *Brooking Papers on Economic Activity, Microeconomics*, 1–38.

Hausman, J. (1998). "Taxation by telecommunications regulation." *Tax Policy and the Economy* 12: 29–48.

Hellwig, M. (2008). "Competition policy and sector-specific regulation for network industries." *Preprints of the Max Planck Institute for Research on Collective Goods*, Bonn, July.

Hesamzadeh, M. R., Rosellón, J., Gabriel, S. A., & Vogelsang, I. (2018). "A simple regulatory incentive mechanism applied to electricity transmission pricing and investment." *Energy Economics* 75: 423–439.

Hoernig, S., & Vogelsang, I. (2013). "The ambivalence of two-part tariffs for bottleneck access." In R. Dewenter, J. Haucap & C. Kehder (eds.). *Wettbewerb und Regulierung in Medien, Politik und Märkten*. Baden-Baden: Nomos, 63–80, http://papers.ssrn.com/sol3/papers.cfm?abstract_id=2176095

Inderst, R., & Peitz, M. (2014). "Investment under uncertainty and regulation of new access networks." *Information Economics and Policy* 26: 28–41.

Katz, M. L., & Shapiro, C. (1985). "Network externalities, competition, and compatibility." *American Economic Review* 75: 424–440.

Koray, S., & Saglam, I. (2005). "The need for regulating a Bayesian regulator." *Journal of Regulatory Economics* 28: 21–28

Krämer, J., & Vogelsang, I. (2016). "Co-investments and tacit collusion in regulated network industries: Experimental evidence." *Review of Network Economics* 15: 35–61.

Laffont, J.-J., & Tirole, J. (1986). "Using Cost Observation to Regulate Firms." *Journal of Political Economy* 94(3): 614-641.

Laffont, J.-J., & Tirole, J. (2000). *Competition in Telecommunications*. Cambridge, MA: MIT Press.

Laffont, J.-J., & Tirole, J. (1993). *A Theory of Incentives in Procurement and Regulation*. Cambridge, MA: MIT Press.

Laffont, J.-J., Rey, P., & Tirole, J. (1998a). "Network competition: I. Overview and nondiscriminatory pricing." *Rand Journal of Economics* 29: 1–37.

Laffont, J.-J., Rey, P., & Tirole, J. (1998b). "Network competition: II. Price discrimination." *Rand Journal of Economics* 29: 38–56.

Lehr, W., & Sicker, D. (2018). "Communications Act 2021." *Journal of High Technology Law* 18(2): 270–330.

Lehr, W., Clark, D. &, Bauer, S. (2019). "Regulation when platforms are layered," 30th European Regional ITS Conference, Helsinki 2019 205193, International Telecommunications Society (ITS).

Liston, C. (1993). "Price-cap versus rate-of-return regulation." *Journal of Regulatory Economics* 5: 25–48.

Littlechild, S. (1983). *Regulation of British Telecommunications Profitability: A Report to the Secretary of State for Trade and Industry*. London.

Littlechild, S. C. (2006). "Mobile termination charges: Calling party pays versus receiving party pays." *Telecommunications Policy* 30: 242–277.

Littlechild, S. (2009). "Stipulated settlements, the consumer advocate and utility regulation in Florida." *Journal of Regulatory Economics* 35: 96–109.

Liu, C., & Jayakar, K. (2012). "The evolution of telecommunications policy-making: Comparative analysis of China and India." *Telecommunications Policy* 36: 13–28.

Loeb, M., & Magat, W. A. (1979). "A decentralized method for utility regulation." *Journal of Law and Economics* 22: 399–404.

Mankiw, N. G., & Whinston, M. D. (1986). "Free entry and social inefficiency." *Rand Journal of Economics* 17: 48–58.

Mitchell, B. M., & Vogelsang, I. (1991). *Telecommunications Pricing: Theory and Practice*. Cambridge, UK: Cambridge University Press.

Musacchio, A., & Lazzarini, S. (2014). *Reinventing State Capitalism: Leviathan in Business*. Cambridge, MA: Harvard University Press.

Nardotto, M., Valetti, T., & Verboven, F. (2015). Unbundling the incumbent: Evidence from UK broadband. *Journal of the European Economic Association* 13: 330–362.

Neumann, K.-H., & Vogelsang, I. (2013). "How to price the unbundled local loop in the transition from copper to fiber access networks?" *Telecommunications Policy* 37: 893–909.

Newbery, D. M. (2018). "What future(s) for liberalized electricity markets: Efficient, equitable, or innovative?" *Energy Journal* 39: 1–27.

Pindyck, R. S. (2007). "Mandatory unbundling and irreversible investment in telecom networks." *Review of Network Economics* 6(3): 1–25.

Riordan, M. H., & Sappington, D. E. M. (1987). "Awarding monopoly franchises." *American Economic Review* 77: 375–387.

Rogerson, W. (2011). "On the relationship between historic cost, forward looking cost and long run marginal cost." *Review of Network Economics* 10(2).

Röller, L. H., & Waverman, L. (2001). "telecommunications infrastructure and economic development: A simultaneous approach." *American Economic Review* 91: 909–923.

Rohlfs, J. (1974). "A theory of interdependent demands for telecommunications services." *Bell Journal of Economics* 5: 16–37.

Sappington, D. E. M., & Sibley, D. S. (1988). "Regulating without cost information: The incremental surplus subsidy scheme." *International Economic Review* 29: 297–306.

Schweppe, F. C., Caramanis, M. C., Tabors, R. B., & Bohn, R. E. (1988). *Spot Pricing of Electricity*. Boston: Kluwer Academic Publishing.

Senyonga, L., & Bergland, O. (2018). "Impact of high-powered incentive regulations on efficiency and productivity growth of Norwegian electric utilities." *Energy Journal* 39: 231–255.

Shaffer, S. (1983). "Demand-side determinants of natural monopoly." *Atlantic Economic Journal* 11: 71–73.

Shapiro, C., & Varian, H. R. (1999). *Information Rules*. Cambridge, MA: Harvard Business School Press.

Sharkey, W. W. (1979). "A decentralized method for utility regulation: A comment." *The Journal of Law and Economics* 22: 405–407.

Shleifer, A., (1985). "A theory of yardstick competition." *Rand Journal of Economics* 16: 319–327.

Spulber, D. F., & Yoo, C. S. (2009). *Networks in Telecommunications: Economics and Law*. Cambridge, UK: Cambridge University Press.

Sutton, J. (1991). *Sunk Costs and Market Structure: Price Competition, Advertising, and the Evolution of Concentration*. Cambridge, MA: MIT Press.

Trillas, F. (2016). "Behavioral regulatory agencies." *Applied Economics Working Papers*, 16–06.

Trillas, F. (2020). "Innovative behavioral regulatory agencies as second generation commitment devices." *Journal of Economic Policy Reform* 23(1): 83–99.

Vickrey, W. (1971). "Responsive Pricing of Public Utility Services." *Bell Journal of Economics* 2: 337–346.

Vogelsang, I. (1984). "Incentive Mechanisms Mimicking German Electric Utility Regulation." Proceedings of the 11th EARIE Conference, Fontainebleau, August 1984, Vol. I: 87–108.

Vogelsang, I. (1989a). "Price cap regulation of telecommunications services: A long-run approach." In M. A. Crew (ed.). *Deregulation and Diversification of Utilities*. Boston: Kluwer Academic Publishers, 21–42.

Vogelsang, I. (1989b). "Two-part tariffs as regulatory constraints." *Journal of Public Economics* 39: 45–66.

Vogelsang, I. (2002). "Incentive regulation and competition in public utility markets: A 20-year perspective." *Journal of Regulatory Economics* 22: 5–28.

Vogelsang, I. (2006). "Electricity transmission pricing and performance-based regulation." *The Energy Journal* 27: 97–126.

Vogelsang, I. (2015). "Will the U.S. and EU telecommunications policies converge? A survey." *Journal of Industrial and Business Economics* (Economia e Politica Industriale) 42: 117–155, http://papers.ssrn.com/sol3/papers.cfm?abstract_id=2463156

Vogelsang, I. (2017a). "Regulatory inertia versus ICT dynamics: The case of product innovations." *Telecommunications Policy* 41: 978–990.

Vogelsang, I. (2017b). "The role of competition and regulation in stimulating innovation – Telecommunications." *Telecommunications Policy* 41: 802–812.

Vogelsang, I. (2018a). "Can simple regulatory mechanisms realistically be used for electricity transmission investment? The case of H-R-G-V." *Economics of Energy & Environmental Policy* 7(1): 63–87.

Vogelsang, I. (2018b). "Net neutrality regulation: Much ado about nothing?" *Review of Network Economics* 17: 225–243.

Vogelsang, I. (2019). "Has Europe missed the endgame of telecommunications policy?" *Telecommunications Policy* 43(1), February: 1–10.

Vogelsang, I. (2020). "A simple merchant-regulatory incentive mechanism applied to electricity transmission pricing and investment: The case of H-R-G-V." Forthcoming in M. R. Hesamzadeh, J. Rosellon, & I. Vogelsang (eds.). *Transmission Network Investment in Liberalized Power Markets.* Springer Verlag, Lecture Notes in Energy.

Vogelsang, I., & Cave, M. (2019). "Framework for promoting competition." Report prepared for the New Zealand Commerce Commission, November.

Vogelsang, I., & Finsinger, J. (1979). "A regulatory adjustment process for optimal pricing by multiproduct monopoly firms." *Bell Journal of Economics* 10: 157–171.

Weiller, C. M., & Pollitt, M. G. (2013). "Platform markets and energy services." EPRGWP 1334, www.eprg.group.cam.ac.uk/wp-content/uploads/2013/12/1334-PDF.pdf

Williamson, O. E. (1975). *Markets and Hierarchies: Analysis and Antitrust Implications.* New York: Free Press.

Williamson, O. E. (1979). "Transaction-cost economics: The governance of contractual relationships." *Journal of Law and Economics* 22: 233–261.

Willig, R. D. (1978). "Pareto-superior nonlinear outlay schedules." *Bell Journal of Economics* 9: 56–69.

Xia, J. (2017). "China's telecommunications evolution, institutions, and policy issues on the eve of 5G: A two-decade retrospect and prospect." *Telecommunications Policy* 41: 931–947.

Yoo, C. (2014). "U.S. vs. European broadband deployment: What do the data say?" www.law.upenn.edu/live/files/3352

Acknowledgements

The author, Professor Ingo Vogelsang, sadly passed away after the submission of his final, revised version of the manuscript. In this final version, the author had duly considered all of the comments by two anonymous reviewers on a previous version. The final version was eventually approved by the series editors. One of the series editors, Professor Massimo Florio, was then in charge of reading the proofs. He was assisted by Dr Paolo Castelnovo (University of Milan) and Ms Martina Gazzo.

Cambridge Elements ⚌

Public Economics

Robin Boadway
Queen's University
Robin Boadway is Emeritus Professor of Economics at Queen's University. His main research interests are in public economics, welfare economics and fiscal federalism.

Frank A. Cowell
The London School of Economics and Political Science
Frank A. Cowell is Professor of Economics at the London School of Economics. His main research interests are in inequality, mobility and the distribution of income and wealth.

Massimo Florio
University of Milan
Massimo Florio is Professor of Public Economics at the University of Milan. His main interests are in cost-benefit analysis, regional policy, privatization, public enterprise, network industries and the socio-economic impact of research infrastructures.

About the series
The Cambridge Elements of Public Economics provides authoritative and up-to-date reviews of core topics and recent developments in the field. It includes state-of-the-art contributions on all areas in the field. The editors are particularly interested in the new frontiers of quantitative methods in public economics, experimental approaches, behavioral public finance, empirical and theoretical analysis of the quality of government and institutions.

Printed in the United States
by Baker & Taylor Publisher Services